HOW TO MANGA
POCKET SIZED! *with* **BEN DUNN**

With Additional text by ROBERT ACOSTA

***Antarctic Press Presents: How to Draw Manga Pocket Manga* Vol. 1, December 2006**, is published by Antarctic Press, 7272 Wurzbach, Suite #204, San Antonio, Texas, 78240. FAX#: (210) 614-5029. Texxt ©2006 Ben Dunn & Robert Acosta. Art ©2006 Ben Dunn. All other material is ™ and ©2006 Antarctic Press. No similarity to any actual person(s) and/or place(s) is intended, and any such similarity is entirely coincidental. Nothing from this book may be reproduced without the express written consent of the authors, except for purposes of review or promotion. *"No, not him! The REAL Gonzo!"* Printed and bound in Canada by Imprimerie Lebonfon, Inc.

For more great "How to DRAW" merchandise, go to:
www.APMANGA.com

BEFORE WE BEGIN

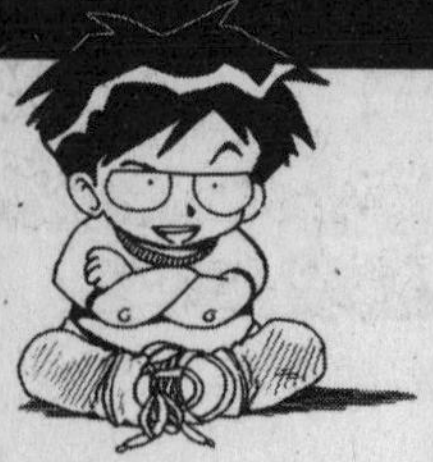

KONNICHIWA! HA! BET YOU DIDN'T THINK I KNEW ANY JAPANESE, DID YOU! ALL KIDDING ASIDE... I DON'T! WHAT I DO KNOW IS THAT I LOVE THE "MANGA" STYLE OF DRAWING! I SAY "MANGA" BECAUSE THERE ARE CERTAIN CHARACTERISTICS THAT SEPARATE IT FROM TRADITIONAL WESTERN COMICS. MORE ON THAT IN LATER CHAPTERS. WHAT I'LL COVER HERE ARE THE ELEMENTS OF MANGA THAT I HAVE CHOSEN TO USE IN MY OWN ART STYLE. I DO NOT PROFESS THIS TO BE THE ONLY WAY TO DO IT, BUT YOU WILL SEE THAT IT USES BASIC ELEMENTS THAT APPLY TO ALL STYLES. SO LET'S NOT WASTE ANY MORE TIME! LET'S ART MANGA!

TOOLS OF THE TRADE!

BEFORE ONE CAN DRAW, ONE MUST HAVE THE RIGHT TOOLS. USE WHAT IS AVAILABLE! ADAPT WITH WHAT YOU KNOW. FOR ME, THE MOST COMMON TOOLS I DRAW WITH ARE: STAEDTLER PIGMENT LINERS (SIZES 01, 03, 05 AND 07), A ZEBRA 0.5 MECHANICAL PENCIL, TYPE HB LEAD, PARALLEL GLIDER RULER, LARGE RAISED-EDGE TRIANGLE, MARS MAGIC RUB ERASER, PEN BRUSH, OPAQUE BLACK INDIA INK, WHITE OUT, WHITE INK, OLD TOOTH-BRUSHES, RAISED-EDGE FRENCH CURVE, VARIOUS CIRCLE AND OVAL TEMPLATES, RAISED-EDGE RULER, FINE-POINT SHARPIE MARKERS, OLD RAGS, TWO LARGE JARS FILLED WITH WATER (ONE FOR CLEANING BLACK INK AND ONE FOR CLEANING WHITE INK), 15-INCH T-SQUARE AND 2-PLY, SMOOTH-SURFACE BRISTOL BOARD. GOT IT? GOOD, LET'S CONTINUE ON.

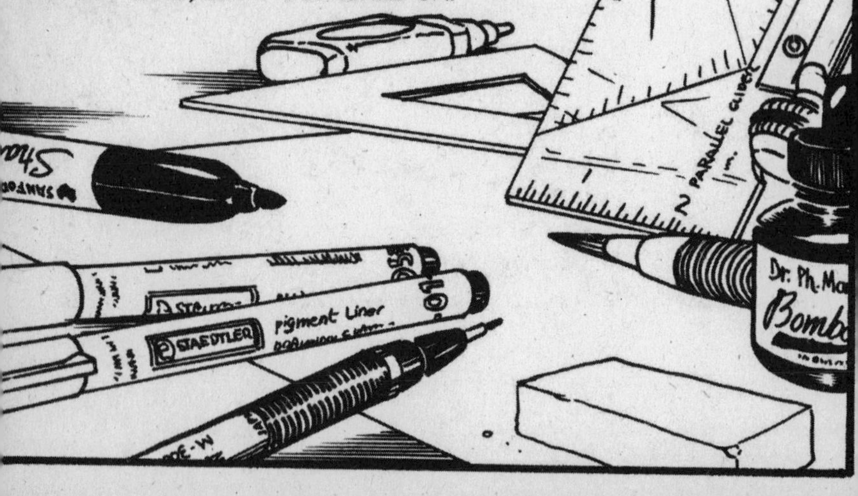
STAEDTLER
pigment Liner

HOW TO DRAW MANGA

BASIC BODY: THE MANNEQUIN

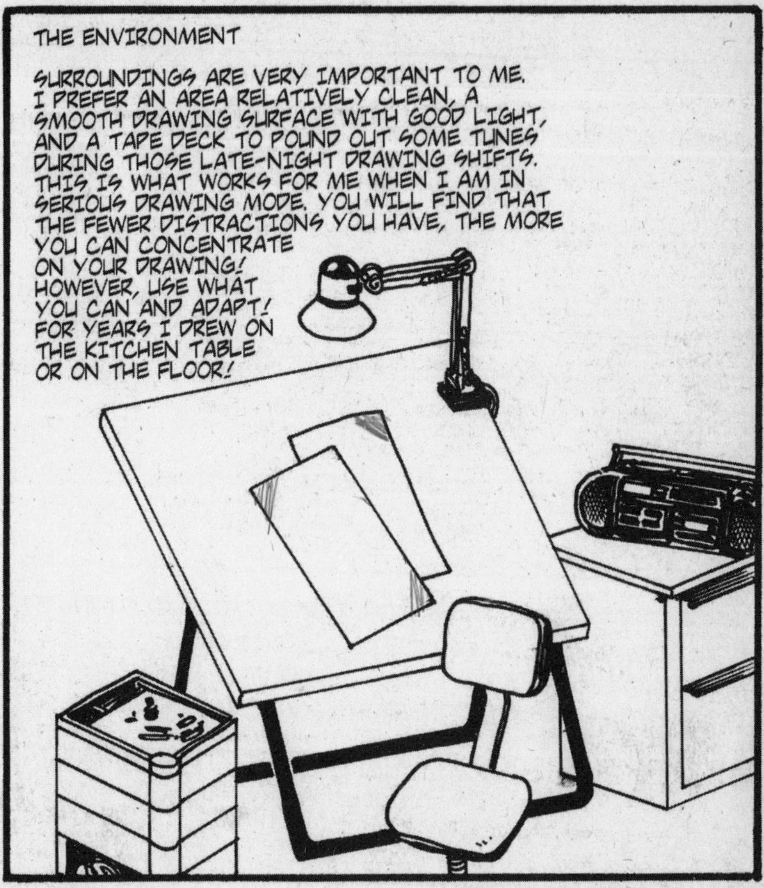
THE ENVIRONMENT
SURROUNDINGS ARE VERY IMPORTANT TO ME. I PREFER AN AREA RELATIVELY CLEAN, A SMOOTH DRAWING SURFACE WITH GOOD LIGHT, AND A TAPE DECK TO POUND OUT SOME TUNES DURING THOSE LATE-NIGHT DRAWING SHIFTS. THIS IS WHAT WORKS FOR ME WHEN I AM IN SERIOUS DRAWING MODE. YOU WILL FIND THAT THE FEWER DISTRACTIONS YOU HAVE, THE MORE YOU CAN CONCENTRATE ON YOUR DRAWING! HOWEVER, USE WHAT YOU CAN AND ADAPT! FOR YEARS I DREW ON THE KITCHEN TABLE OR ON THE FLOOR!

HOW TO DRAW MANGA

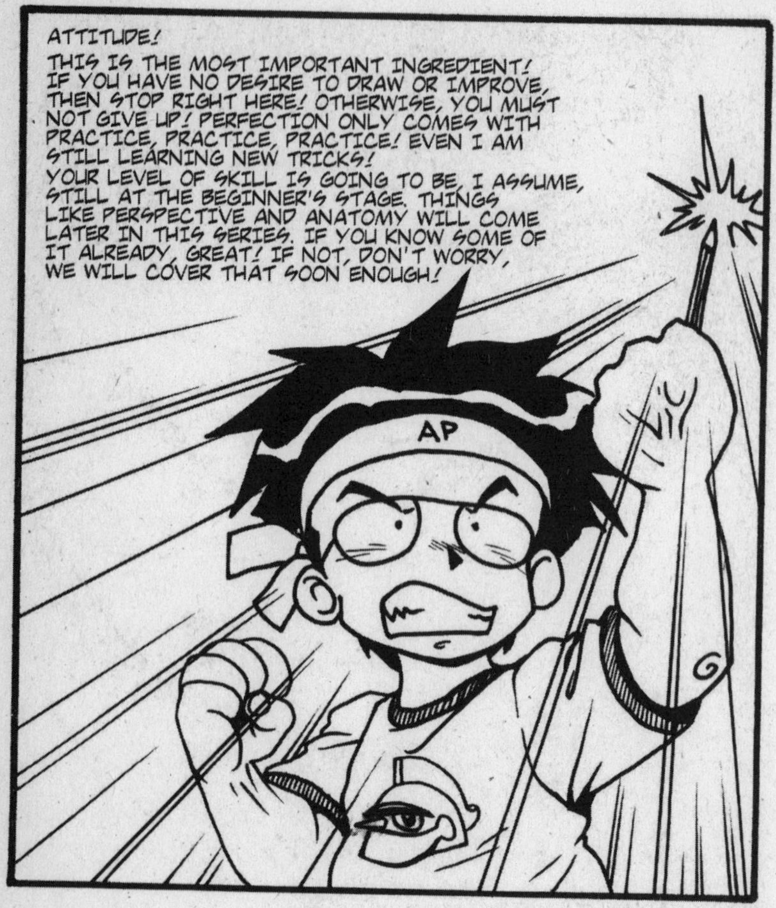
ATTITUDE!
THIS IS THE MOST IMPORTANT INGREDIENT! IF YOU HAVE NO DESIRE TO DRAW OR IMPROVE, THEN STOP RIGHT HERE! OTHERWISE, YOU MUST NOT GIVE UP! PERFECTION ONLY COMES WITH PRACTICE, PRACTICE, PRACTICE! EVEN I AM STILL LEARNING NEW TRICKS!
YOUR LEVEL OF SKILL IS GOING TO BE, I ASSUME, STILL AT THE BEGINNER'S STAGE. THINGS LIKE PERSPECTIVE AND ANATOMY WILL COME LATER IN THIS SERIES. IF YOU KNOW SOME OF IT ALREADY, GREAT! IF NOT, DON'T WORRY, WE WILL COVER THAT SOON ENOUGH!
AP

HOW TO DRAW MANGA

BASIC BODY: THE MANNEQUIN

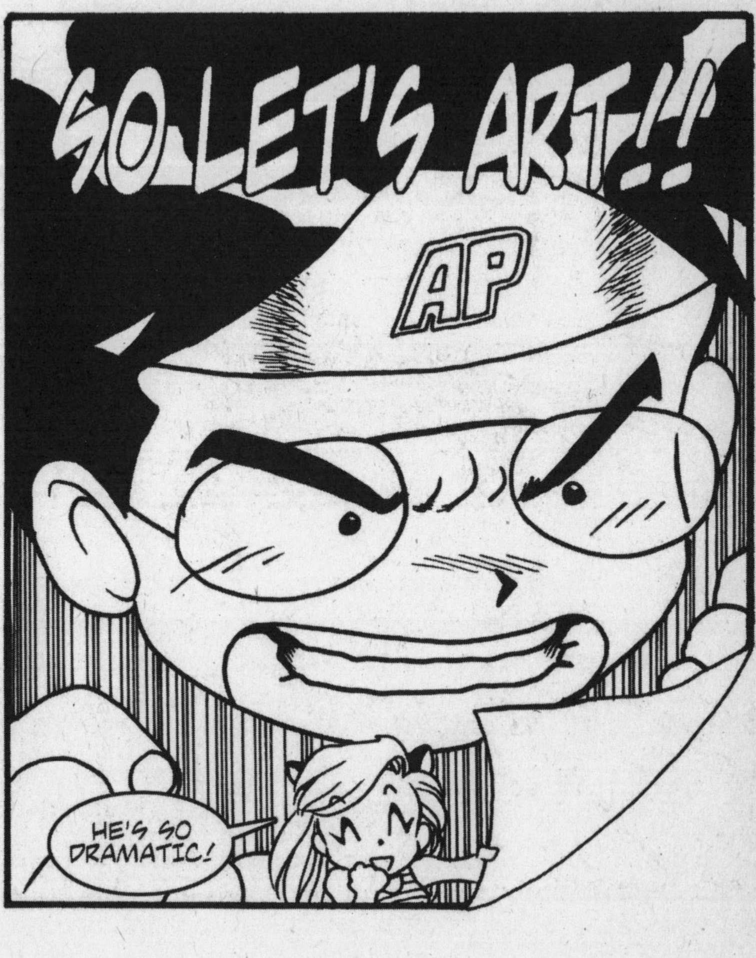
SO LET'S ART!!
AP
HE'S SO DRAMATIC!

HOW TO DRAW MANGA

BASIC BODY: THE MANNEQUIN

MY BASIC HUMAN STRUCTURE FOR THE AVERAGE NINJA HIGH SCHOOL CHARACTER BEGINS WITH WHAT I CALL THE "BALL AND SOCKET MANNEQUIN." ESSENTIALLY, THE BODY AND ITS JOINTS ARE SIMPLIFIED TO THE POINT WHERE THEY ARE SHOWN AS BALL AND SOCKETS.

HEAD AND SHOULDERS: THE HEAD IS CONNECTED AT THE BASE OF THE NECK SOCKET. YOU SHOULD TRY TO FOLLOW THE NATURAL MOVEMENT OF THE HEAD AS IT RELATES TO THE NECK AND SHOULDERS.

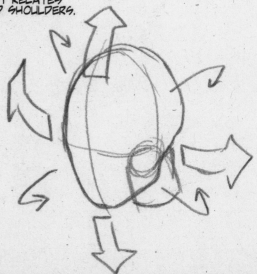

BASIC BODY: THE MANNEQUIN

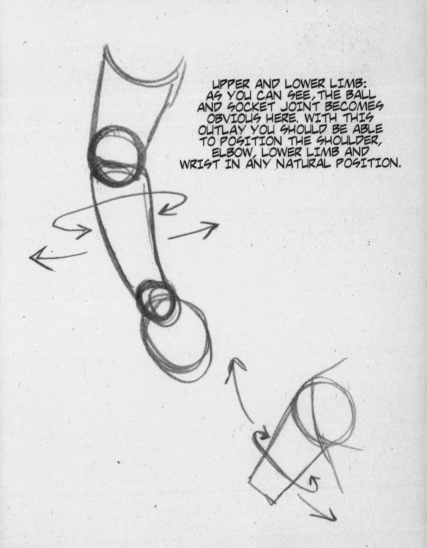

UPPER AND LOWER LIMB:
AS YOU CAN SEE, THE BALL
AND SOCKET JOINT BECOMES
OBVIOUS HERE. WITH THIS
OUTLAY YOU SHOULD BE ABLE
TO POSITION THE SHOULDER,
ELBOW, LOWER LIMB AND
WRIST IN ANY NATURAL POSITION.

BASIC BODY: THE MANNEQUIN

CHEST AND UPPER
ABDOMEN:
AN OVAL BALL FITS
NICELY BETWEEN THE
UPPER RIB CAGE AND
THE LOWER ABDOMEN.
SLIDING IT AROUND,
YOU CAN DRAW THE
BODY IN NATURAL
STANCES WITHOUT
IT LOOKING AWKWARD.

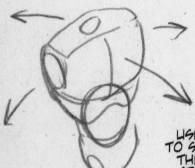

USE THE CENTER AXIS
TO SHOW THE SPINE AND
THEN DRAW THE BODY
AROUND THAT SPINE!

BASIC BODY: THE MANNEQUIN

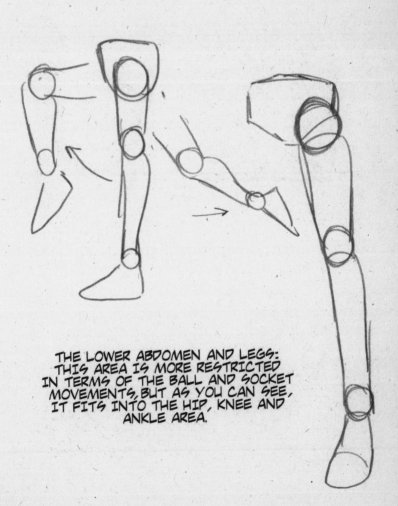

THE LOWER ABDOMEN AND LEGS:
THIS AREA IS MORE RESTRICTED
IN TERMS OF THE BALL AND SOCKET
MOVEMENTS, BUT AS YOU CAN SEE,
IT FITS INTO THE HIP, KNEE AND
ANKLE AREA.

HOW TO DRAW MANGA

BASIC BODY: THE MANNEQUIN

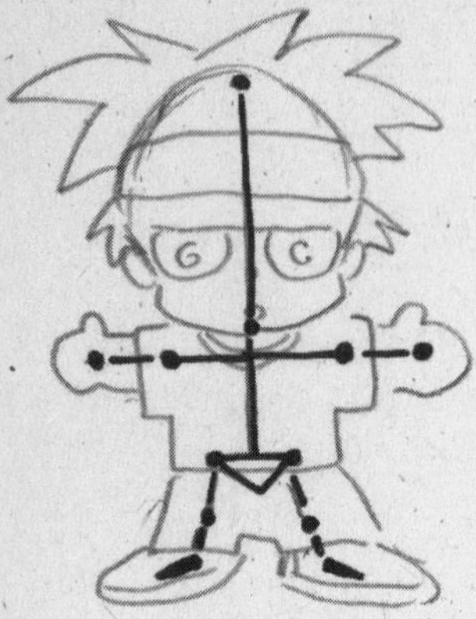

DRAWING SECRET:
IF YOU REMEMBER THE BODY AS A SERIES OF INTERNAL PIPE BONES, YOU CAN PLAN THE STRUCTURE OF THE BODY EARLY AND THEN DRAW AROUND IT.

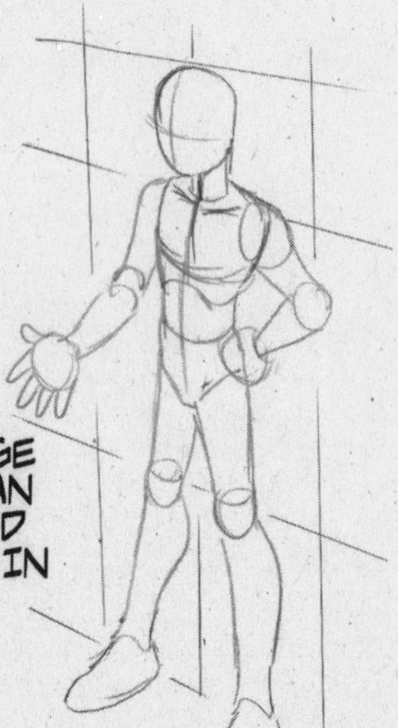

BY USING THE KNOWLEDGE OF PERSPECTIVE, YOU CAN USE THE MANNEQUIN AND PLACE YOUR CHARACTER IN MORE DRAMATIC AND EXCITING WAYS!

HOW TO DRAW MANGA

BASIC BODY: THE MANNEQUIN

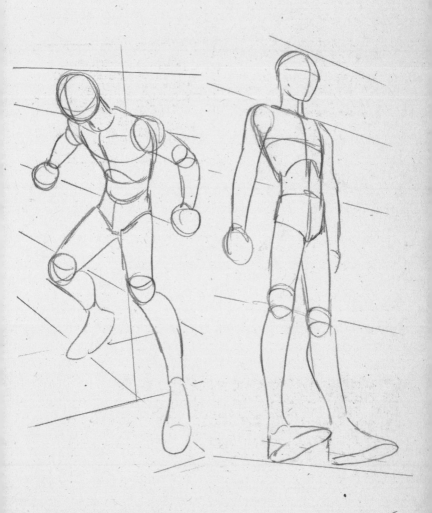

BASIC BODY: THE MANNEQUIN

ONCE YOU'VE MASTERED THE MANNEQUIN FORM, YOU CAN DRAW YOUR CHARACTERS IN ANY POSITION IMAGINABLE!

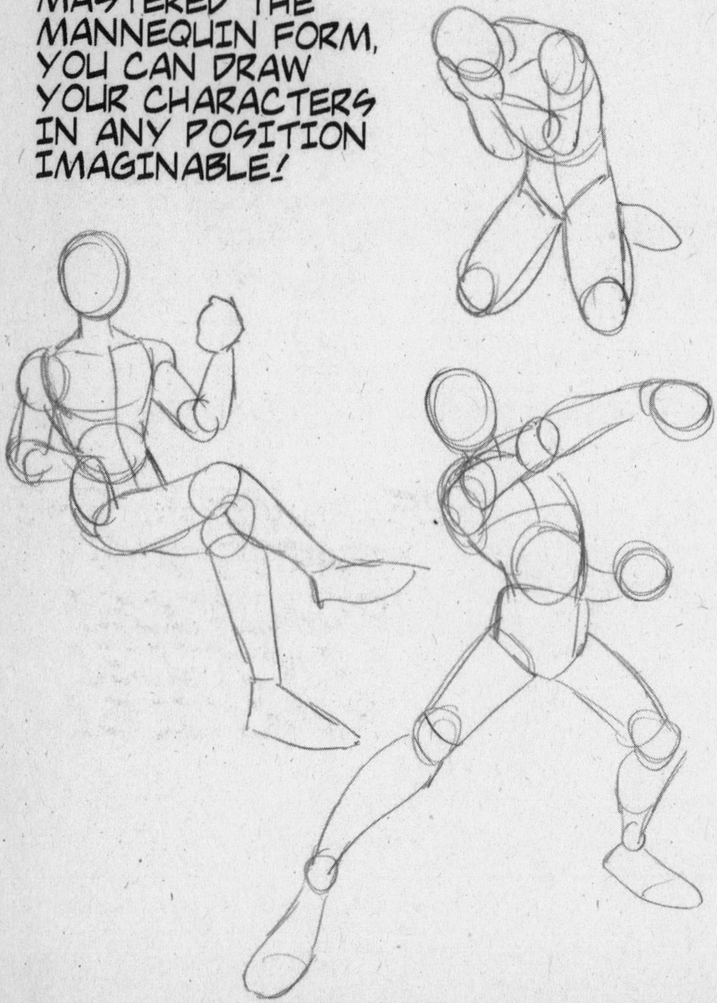

HOW TO DRAW MANGA

BASIC BODY: THE MANNEQUIN

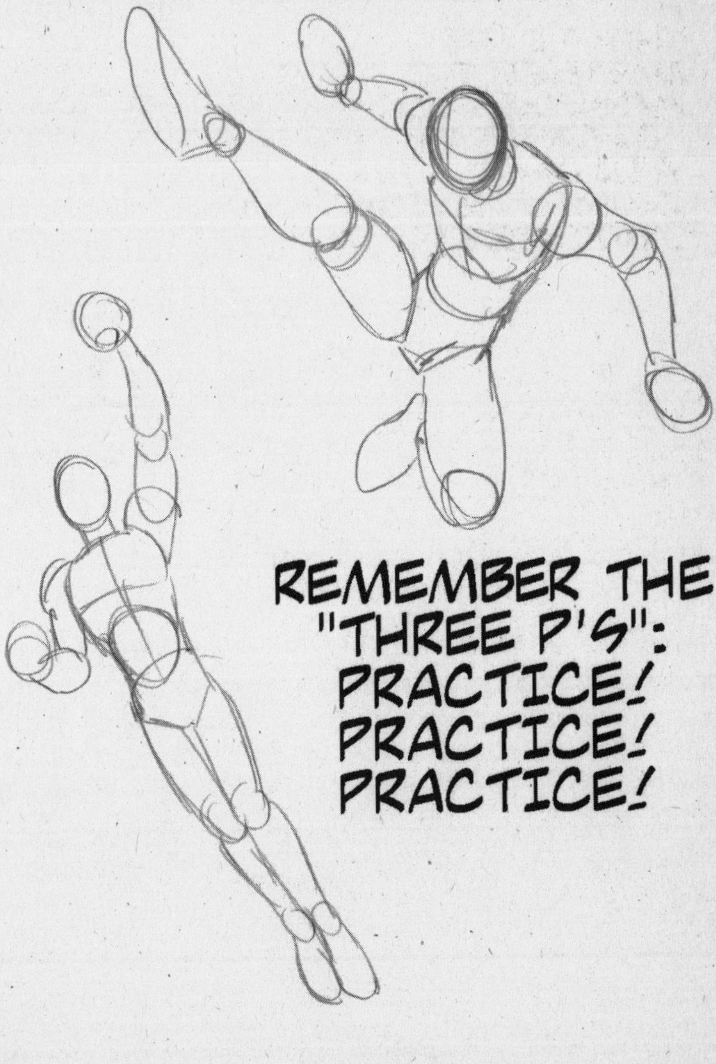

REMEMBER THE "THREE P'S": PRACTICE! PRACTICE! PRACTICE!

HOW TO DRAW MANGA

BASIC BODY: THE MANNEQUIN

ALL RIGHT, THEN. NOW THAT WE'VE PRACTICED DRAWING FIGURES USING THE MANNEQUIN TECHNIQUE. LET US GET INTO WHAT IT TAKES TO DRAW A TYPICAL NINJA HIGH SCHOOL CHARACTER. FOR THE MOST PART, THE BASIC BODY STRUCTURE IS THE SAME FOR A MAJORITY OF NINJA HIGH SCHOOL CHARACTERS. THE THING THAT SEPARATES THEM IS THE WINDOW DRESSING. HOWEVER, LET ME REVIEW THE MALE AND FEMALE BODY STRUCTURES OF NHS.

THE AVERAGE NHS MALE IS VERY WIRY WITH THIN ARMS AND THIN LEGS. HE IS ALSO ABOUT 5 1/2 HEADS TALL. THE BODY IS VERY STRAIGHT WITH ALMOST NO CURVES. HANDS AND FEET TEND TO BE A LITTLE BIGGER THAN NORMAL IN ORDER TO EMPHASIZE MOVEMENT.

FEMALE

MALE

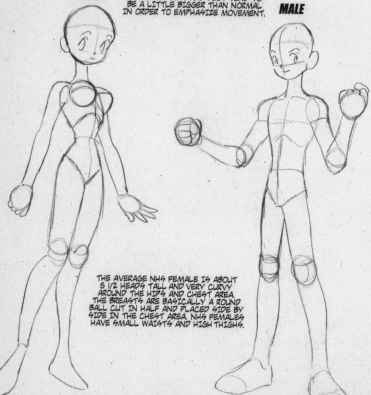

THE AVERAGE NHS FEMALE IS ABOUT 5 1/2 HEADS TALL AND VERY CURVY AROUND THE HIPS AND CHEST AREA. THE BREASTS ARE BASICALLY A ROUND BALL CUT IN HALF AND PLACED SIDE BY SIDE IN THE CHEST AREA. NHS FEMALES HAVE SMALL WAISTS AND HIGH THIGHS.

PRACTICE PAGE

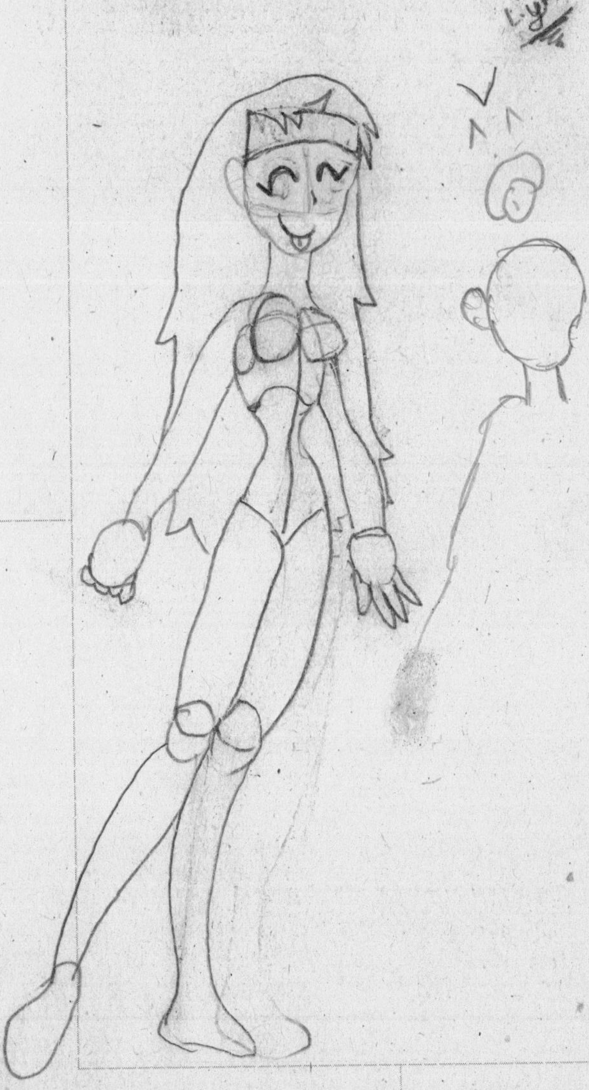

HOW TO DRAW MANGA

DRAWING THE HEAD

NOW WE BEGIN TO CONSTRUCT THE FIGURE.
I USUALLY START WITH THE HEAD BEFORE
I DO THE REST OF THE BODY. LET'S PRACTICE
A LITTLE WITH THE HEAD, SHALL WE?

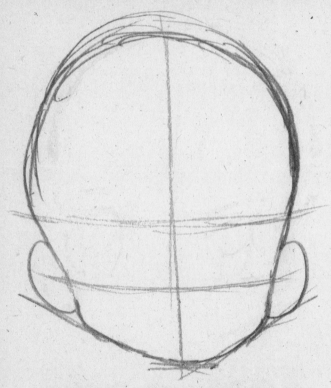

START A CIRCLE AND SKETCH
A LOWER JAW AROUND IT.
PENCIL IN THE EYE AREA,
NOSE AREA, AND MOUTH AREA.

HOW TO DRAW MANGA
DRAWING THE HEAD
STEP TWO

NOW FILL IN THE AREAS
WITH THE ESSENTIAL
FACE PARTS. UP TO HERE,
MOST NHS CHARACTERS
LOOK THE SAME.

HOW TO DRAW MANGA

DRAWING THE HEAD

STEP THREE

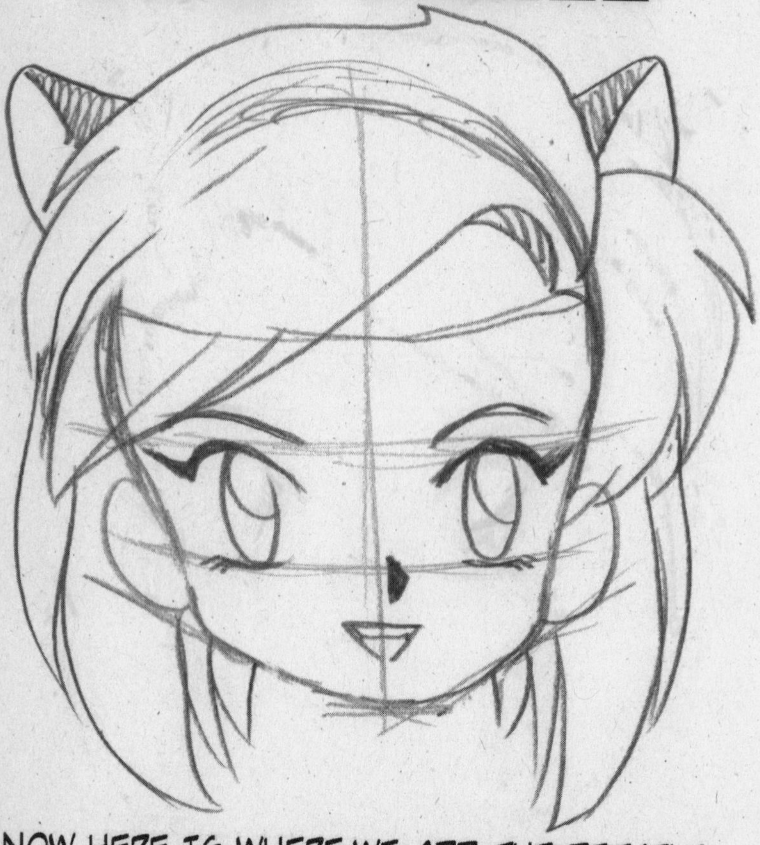

NOW HERE IS WHERE WE ADD THE DETAILS. I'VE ADDED A HAIRLINE SO I KNOW WHERE THE HAIR WILL FALL.

HOW TO DRAW MANGA

DRAWING THE HEAD

STEP FOUR

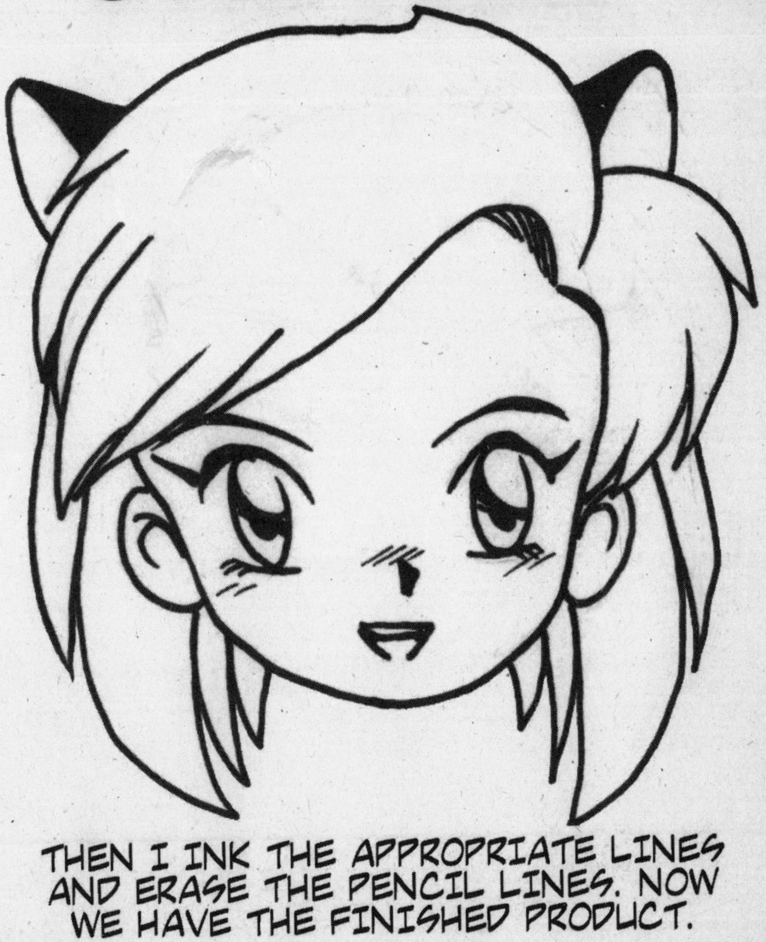

THEN I INK THE APPROPRIATE LINES AND ERASE THE PENCIL LINES. NOW WE HAVE THE FINISHED PRODUCT.

PRACTICE PAGE

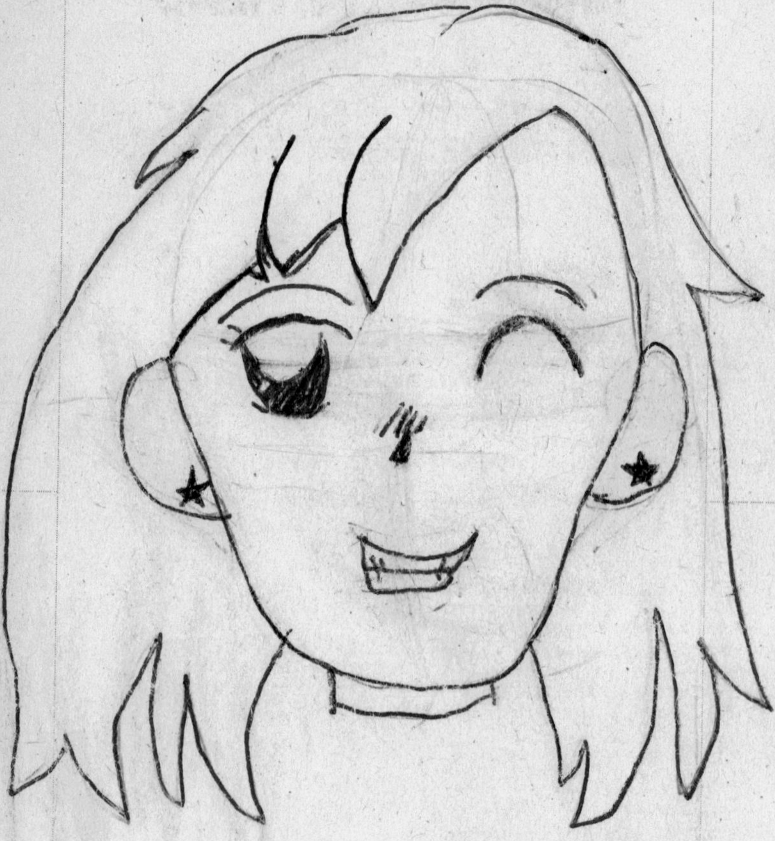

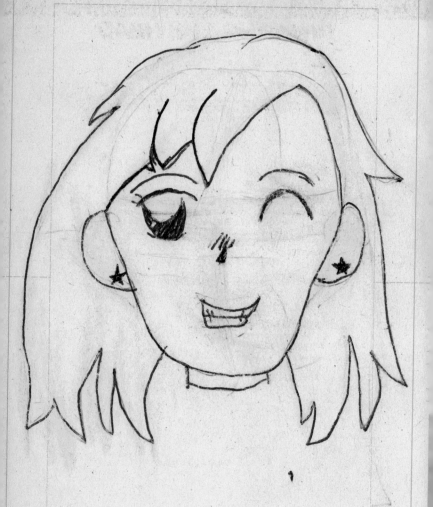

HOW TO DRAW MANGA

DRAWING THE HEAD

NOW LET'S TRY THE HEAD AT A SLIGHTLY DIFFERENT ANGLE.

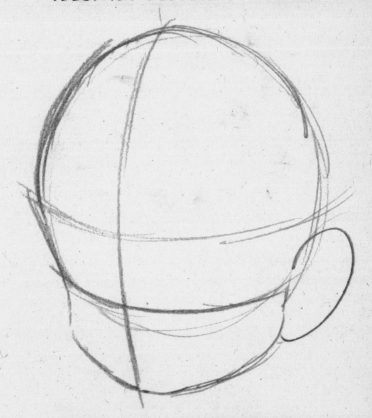

START WITH A CIRCLE AND WORK IN THE BASIC FACE STRUCTURE.

DRAWING THE HEAD

STEP TWO

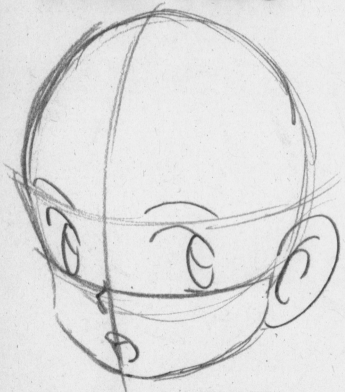

ADD IN EYES, NOSE AND MOUTH.

HOW TO DRAW MANGA

DRAWING THE HEAD

STEP THREE

ADD HAIRLINE AND
BEGIN TO ADD DETAILS
TO THE FACE TO MAKE IT
UNIQUE.

HOW TO DRAW MANGA

DRAWING THE HEAD

STEP FOUR

ERASE THE PENCILS,
AND VOILA! YOU'RE
DOING GREAT!

PRACTICE PAGE

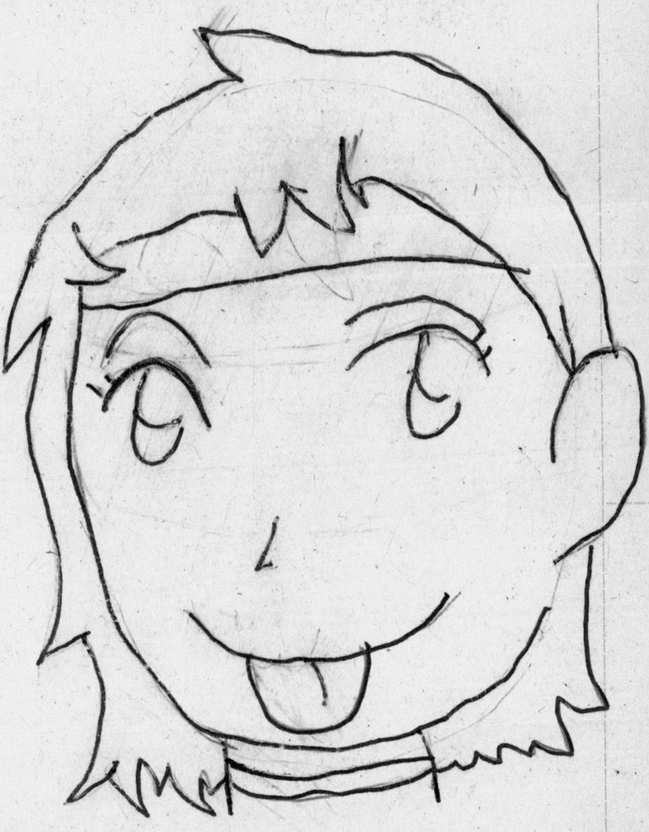

HOW TO DRAW MANGA

DRAWING THE HEAD

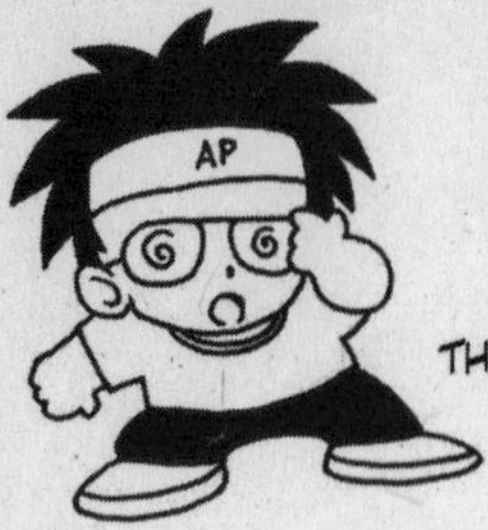
AP

THE HEAD IS PERHAPS THE MOST IMPORTANT PART OF THE BODY IN TERMS OF ARTISTIC EXPRESSION. IT IS THIS PART THAT MOST PEOPLE SEE EVERYDAY, AND IN MANGA THE HEAD SAYS EVERYTHING ABOUT THE CHARACTER! TRY DESIGNING YOUR OWN CHARACTERS STARTING WITH THE HEAD AND SEE WHAT YOU COME UP WITH!

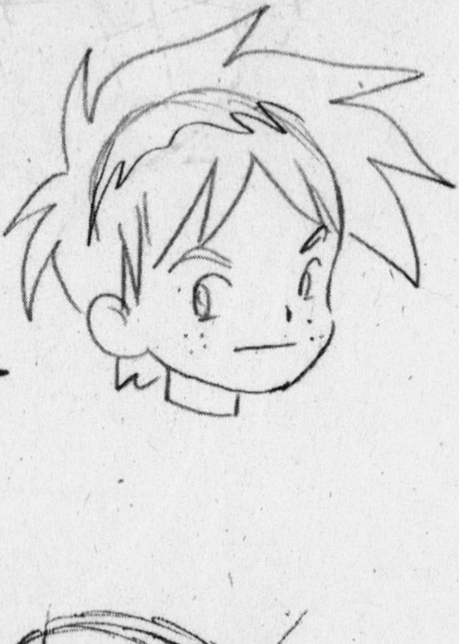

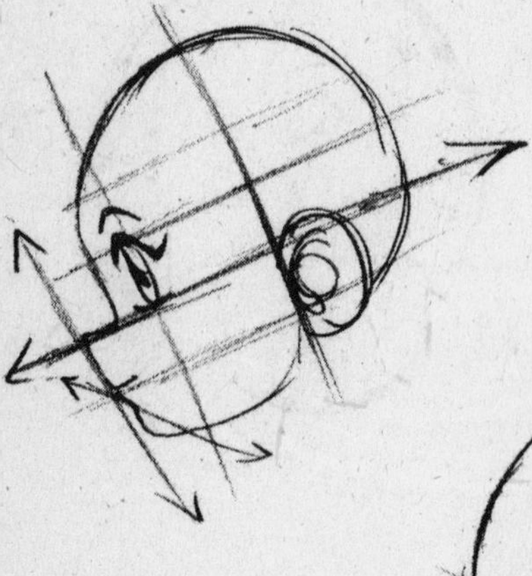

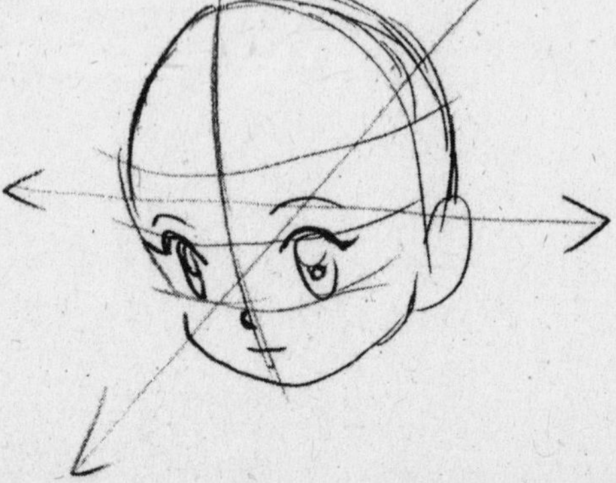

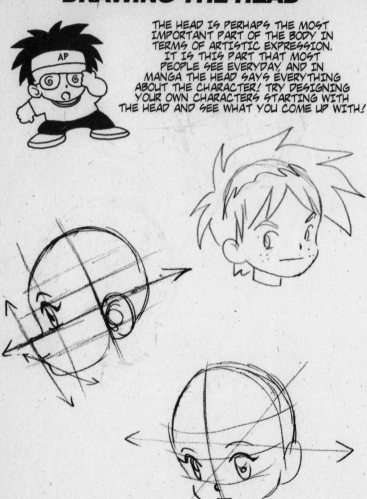

HOW TO DRAW MANGA

DRAWING THE HEAD

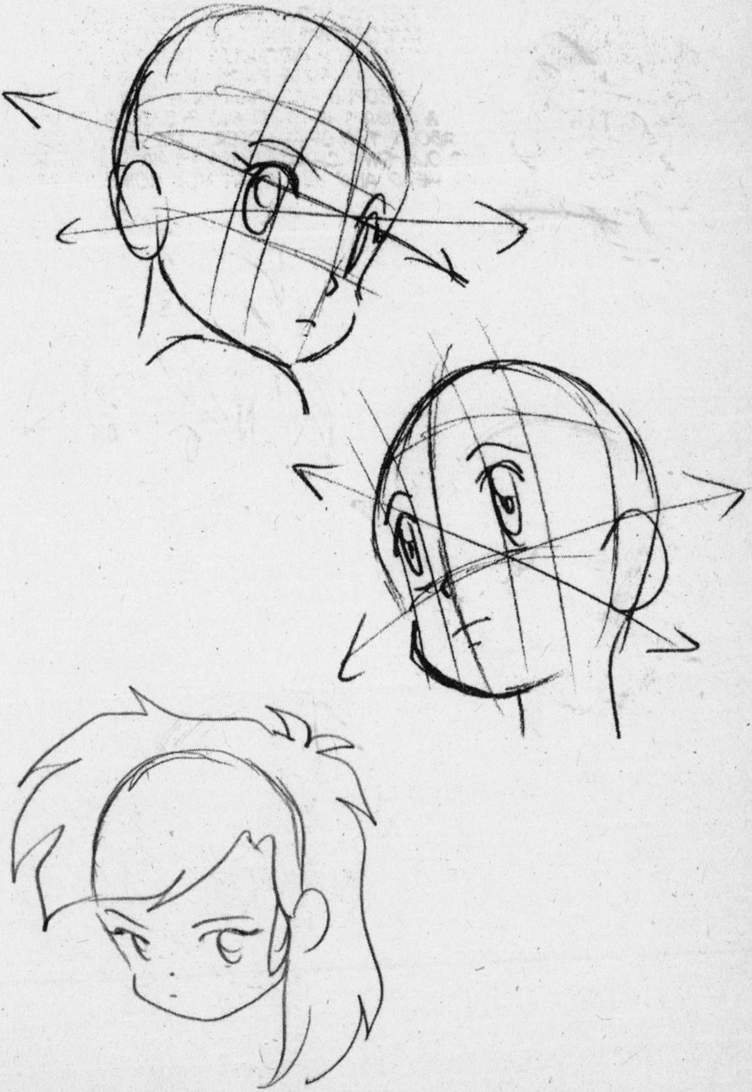

HOW TO DRAW MANGA

DRAWING THE HEAD

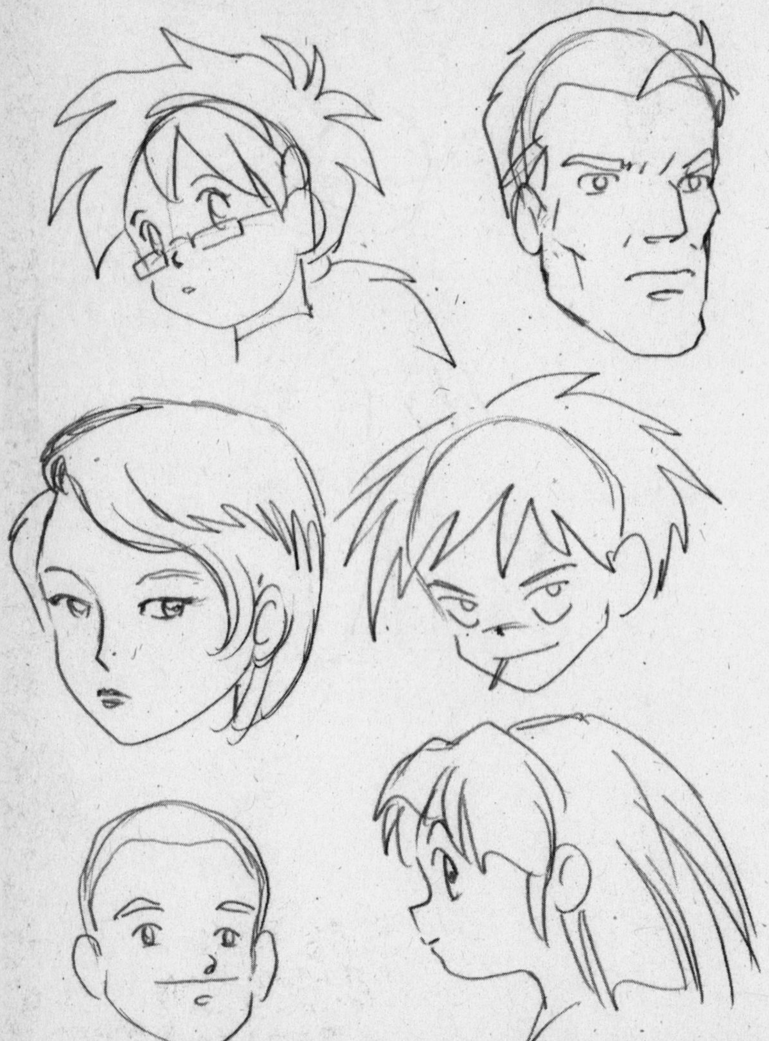

LET'S DRAW A FIGURE!

1

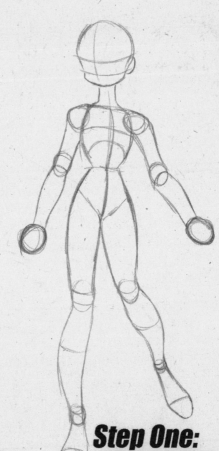

**Step One:
Doing the
basic outline.**

HOW TO DRAW MANGA

LET'S DRAW A FIGURE!

2

**Step Two:
Adding in
the details.**

HOW TO DRAW MANGA

LET'S DRAW A FIGURE!

3

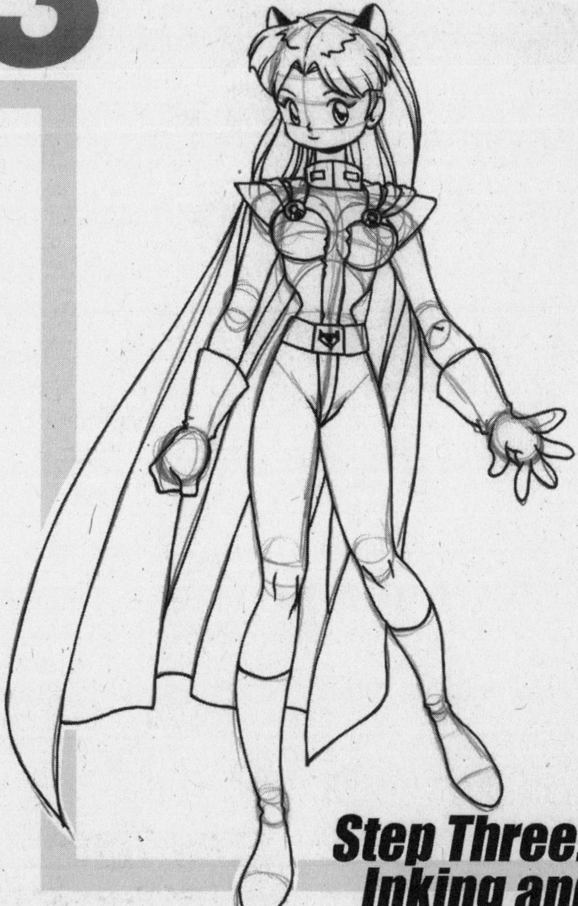

Step Three: Inking and rendering the figure.

HOW TO DRAW MANGA

LET'S DRAW A FIGURE!

4

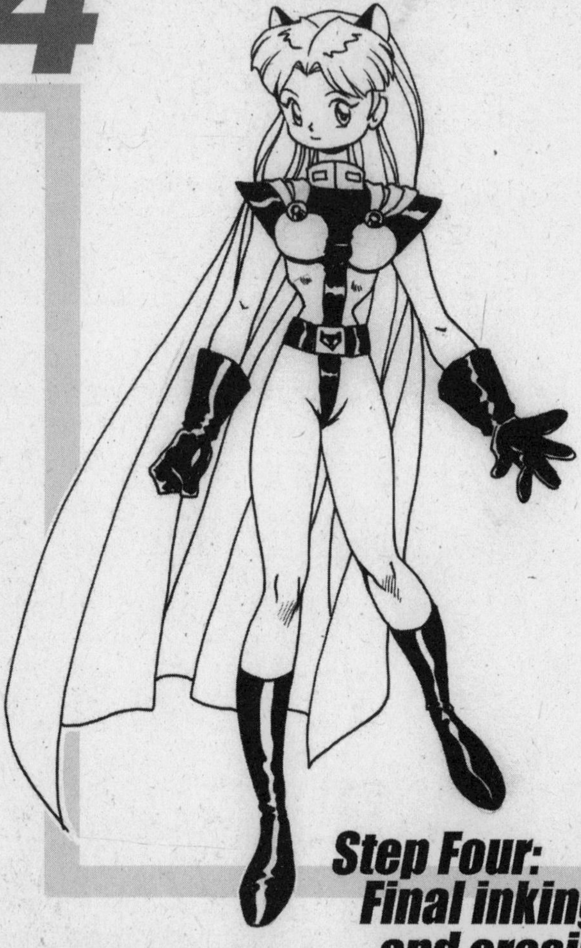

Step Four: Final inking and erasing.

PRACTICE PAGE

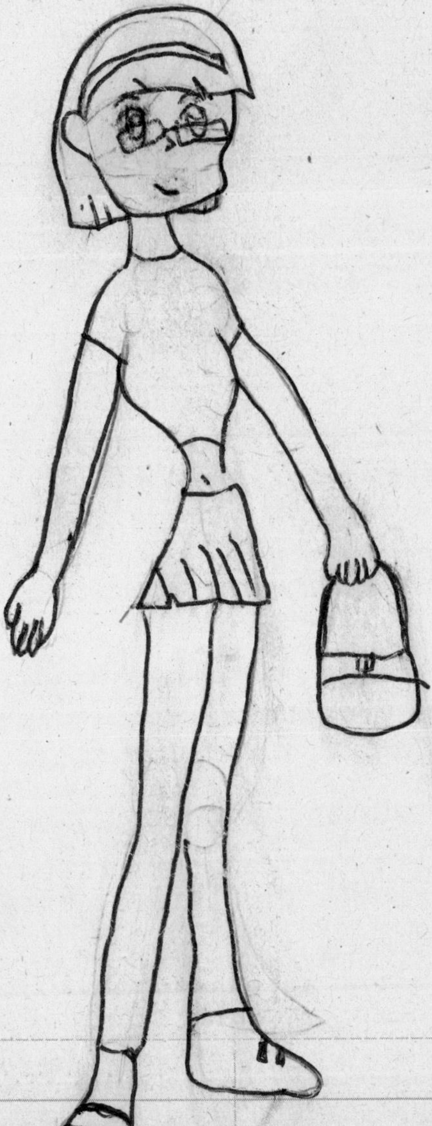

HOW TO DRAW MANGA

BODY LANGUAGE

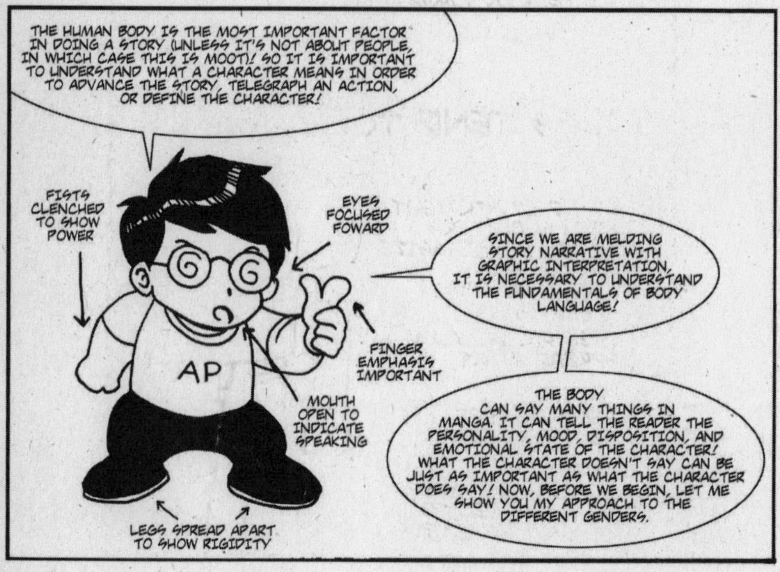

THE HUMAN BODY IS THE MOST IMPORTANT FACTOR IN DOING A STORY (UNLESS IT'S NOT ABOUT PEOPLE, IN WHICH CASE THIS IS MOOT)! SO IT IS IMPORTANT TO UNDERSTAND WHAT A CHARACTER MEANS IN ORDER TO ADVANCE THE STORY, TELEGRAPH AN ACTION, OR DEFINE THE CHARACTER!
FISTS CLENCHED TO SHOW POWER
EYES FOCUSED FOWARD
SINCE WE ARE MELDING STORY NARRATIVE WITH GRAPHIC INTERPRETATION, IT IS NECESSARY TO UNDERSTAND THE FUNDAMENTALS OF BODY LANGUAGE!
AP
FINGER EMPHASIS IMPORTANT
MOUTH OPEN TO INDICATE SPEAKING
THE BODY CAN SAY MANY THINGS IN MANGA. IT CAN TELL THE READER THE PERSONALITY, MOOD, DISPOSITION, AND EMOTIONAL STATE OF THE CHARACTER! WHAT THE CHARACTER DOESN'T SAY CAN BE JUST AS IMPORTANT AS WHAT THE CHARACTER DOES SAY! NOW, BEFORE WE BEGIN, LET ME SHOW YOU MY APPROACH TO THE DIFFERENT GENDERS.
LEGS SPREAD APART TO SHOW RIGIDITY

BODY LANGUAGE

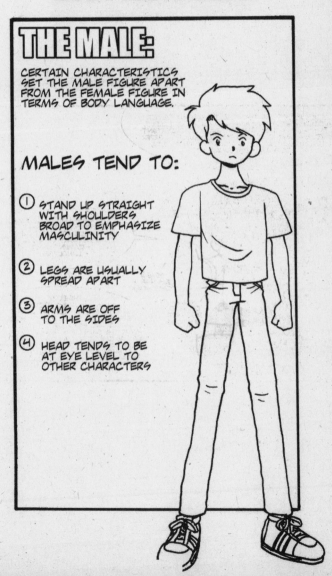

THE MALE:

CERTAIN CHARACTERISTICS
SET THE MALE FIGURE APART
FROM THE FEMALE FIGURE IN
TERMS OF BODY LANGUAGE.

MALES TEND TO:

1. STAND UP STRAIGHT
   WITH SHOULDERS
   BROAD TO EMPHASIZE
   MASCULINITY

2. LEGS ARE USUALLY
   SPREAD APART

3. ARMS ARE OFF
   TO THE SIDES

4. HEAD TENDS TO BE
   AT EYE LEVEL TO
   OTHER CHARACTERS

THE FEMALE:

THE CHARACTERISTICS OF
THIS GENDER ARE THAT
THEY ARE SOFT AND CURVY.

FEMALES TEND TO:

1. SHOULDERS TEND TO BE A LITTLE MORE RELAXED

2. THE FIGURE TENDS TO CURVE OFF CENTER

3. ARMS ARE CLOSER TO THE BODY

4. LEGS ARE USUALLY CLOSER TOGETHER

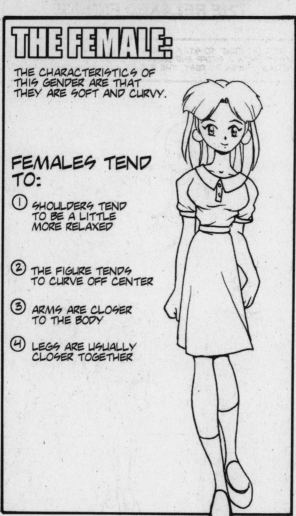

BODY LANGUAGE
THE RELAXED FIGURE

BODIES AT REST TEND TO STAY AT REST. WHEN DRAWING THE FIGURE AT REST, DON'T SHOW A STIFF AND UNNATURAL FIGURE, BUT SHOW A FIGURE REALLY AT REST! EVEN AT REST, THE FIGURE CAN BE SHOWN DRAMATICALLY!

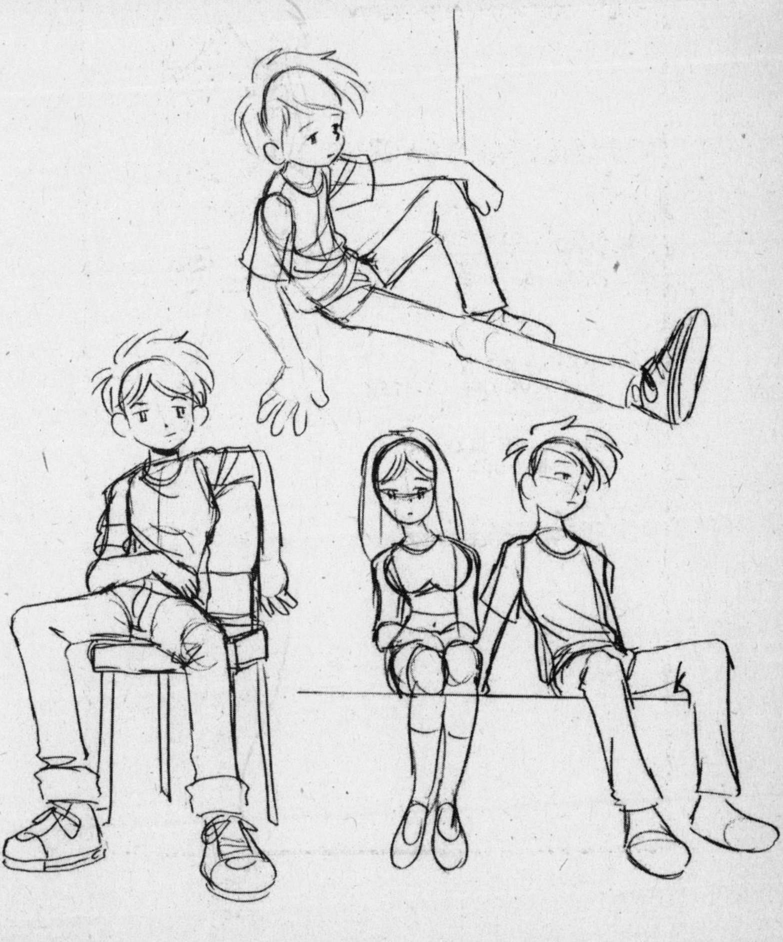

HOW TO DRAW MANGA

BODY LANGUAGE
THE RELAXED FIGURE

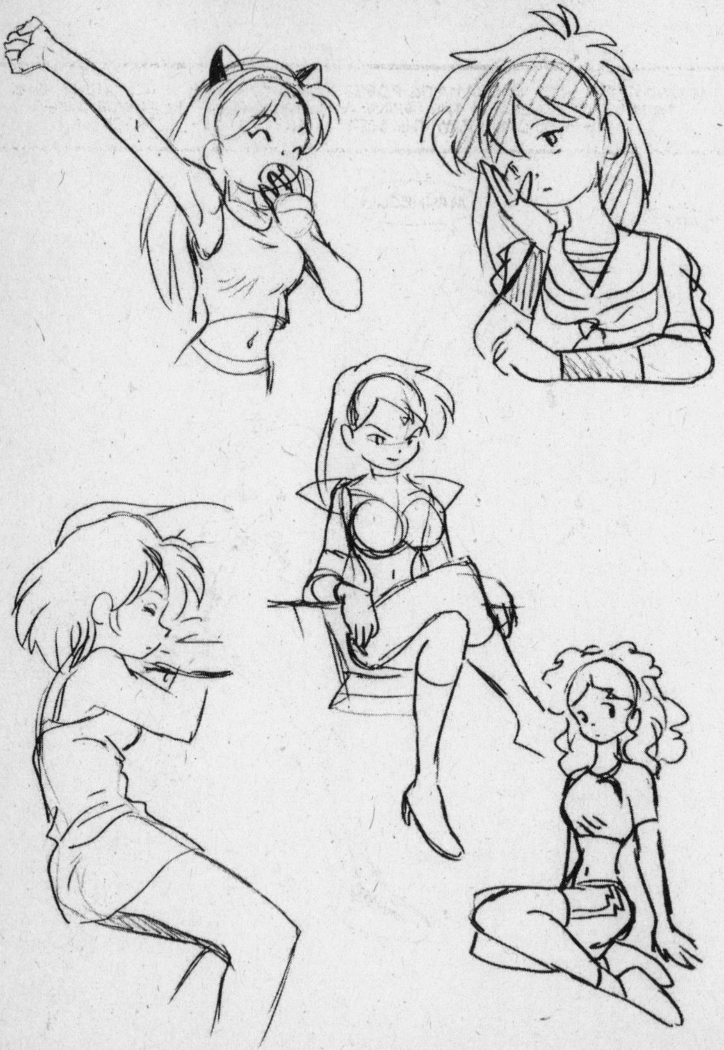

HOW TO DRAW MANGA

BODY LANGUAGE
THE BODY IN MOTION

> SHOWING THE BODY IN DRAMATIC POSES IS WHAT MANGA IS ALL ABOUT. ONE TRICK TO REMEMBER IS THE "SPINE AND MANNEQUIN" TECHNIQUE. WITH THIS, YOU CAN DRAW THE BODY IN ALMOST ANY POSITION.

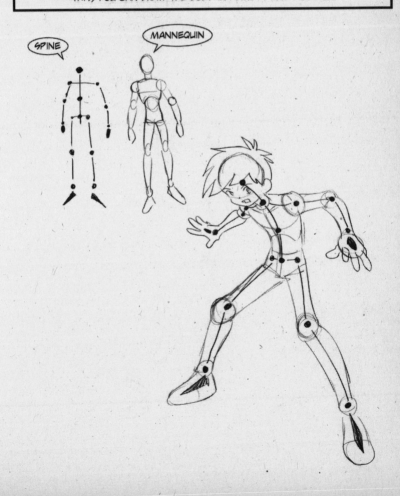

SPINE

MANNEQUIN

BODY LANGUAGE
THE BODY IN MOTION

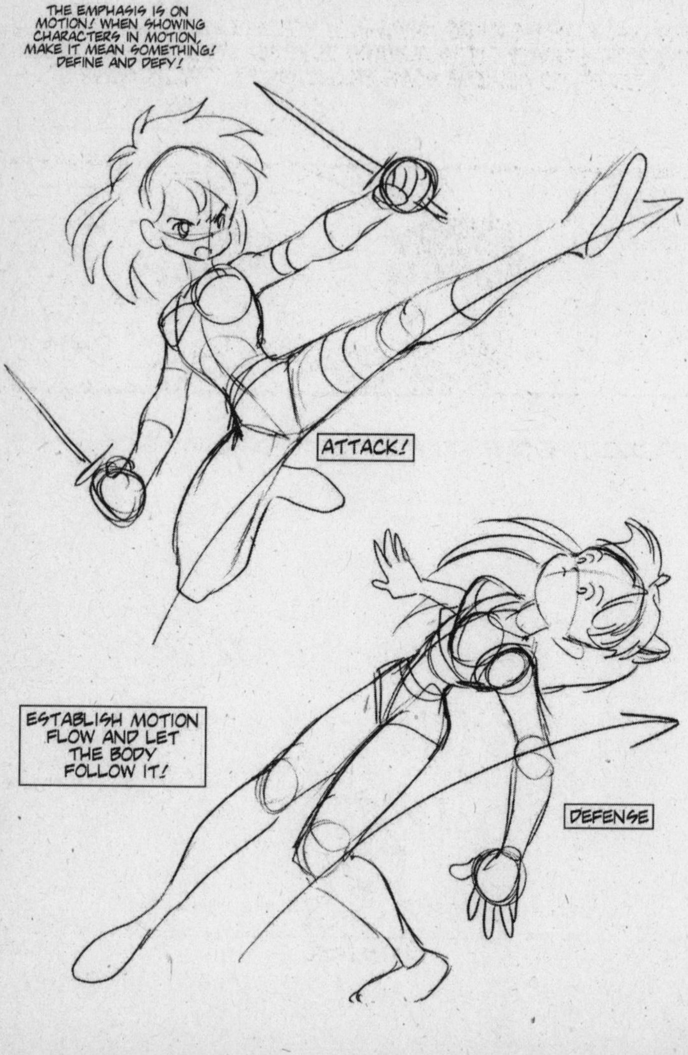
THE EMPHASIS IS ON MOTION! WHEN SHOWING CHARACTERS IN MOTION, MAKE IT MEAN SOMETHING! DEFINE AND DEFY!
ATTACK!
ESTABLISH MOTION FLOW AND LET THE BODY FOLLOW IT!
DEFENSE

HOW TO DRAW MANGA

BODY LANGUAGE
FIGHT SCENES

IN MANGA, BODIES CAN DO ANYTHING! YOU ARE NOT LIMITED BY TIME, SPACE, OR GRAVITY! IT IS ALWAYS BEST TO "FOLLOW THE FLOW" IN ORDER TO ACHIEVE SOME BELIEVABILITY. FOR EXAMPLE:

ICHI IS PISSED OFF AT ASRIAL AND WANTS TO KICK HER BUTT!
YOU TOOK THE LAST TWINKIE!
PREPARE TO DIE!

ICHI DECIDES TO DO A STANDARD RUNNING ATTACK!

FLOW OF BODY
FLOW OF ACTION
START
GROUND LEVEL
CONTINUE →

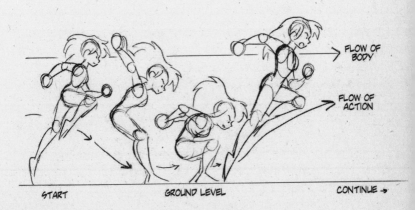

HOW TO DRAW MANGA

BODY LANGUAGE
FIGHT SCENES

CONTINUE →

VICTIM →

FINISH

OF COURSE ASRIAL WOULDN'T SIMPLY LET ICHI ATTACK HER,
SO SHE WILL DEFEND IN A WAY THAT WOULD COUNTER
ICHI'S FLYING ATTACK!

HOW TO DRAW MANGA

BODY LANGUAGE

FIGHT SCENES

THERE ARE MANY WAYS THAT ASRIAL COULD COUNTER ICHI'S ATTACK!

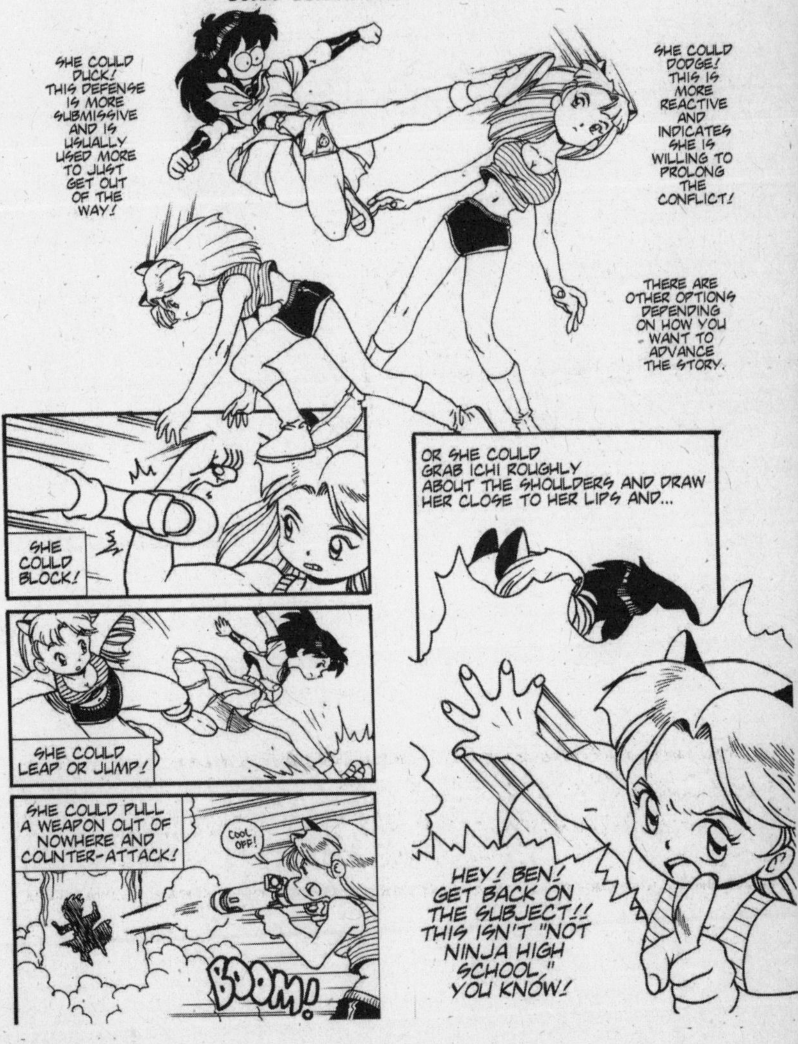

SHE COULD DUCK! THIS DEFENSE IS MORE SUBMISSIVE AND IS USUALLY USED MORE TO JUST GET OUT OF THE WAY!
SHE COULD DODGE! THIS IS MORE REACTIVE AND INDICATES SHE IS WILLING TO PROLONG THE CONFLICT!
THERE ARE OTHER OPTIONS DEPENDING ON HOW YOU WANT TO ADVANCE THE STORY.
SHE COULD BLOCK!
SHE COULD LEAP OR JUMP!
SHE COULD PULL A WEAPON OUT OF NOWHERE AND COUNTER-ATTACK!
COOL OFF!
BOOM!
OR SHE COULD GRAB ICHI ROUGHLY ABOUT THE SHOULDERS AND DRAW HER CLOSE TO HER LIPS AND...
HEY! BEN! GET BACK ON THE SUBJECT!! THIS ISN'T "NOT NINJA HIGH SCHOOL," YOU KNOW!

HOW TO DRAW MANGA

BODY LANGUAGE
FIGHT SCENES

AHEM... YES. WELL, YOU GET THE IDEA. THE NAME OF THE GAME IS MOVEMENT, OR AT LEAST THE IDEA OF MOVEMENT. SINCE MANGA IS A STATIC, TWO-DIMENSIONAL MEDIUM, YOU HAVE TO GIVE THE READER THE IDEA THAT YOUR CHARACTERS ARE MOVING WHEN THEY ARE NOT. SINCE NHS IS A HUMOR BOOK, THE FIGHT SCENES TEND TO BE MORE OUTRAGEOUS. HERE ARE SOME STANDARD STOCK FIGHT SCENES I TEND TO EMPLOY. ALLOW ICHI TO DEMONSTRATE AS LENDO VOLUNTEERS.

STAR FOR EFFECT

THE "ONE FOOT IN THE FACE"

HOW TO DRAW MANGA

BODY LANGUAGE
FIGHT SCENES

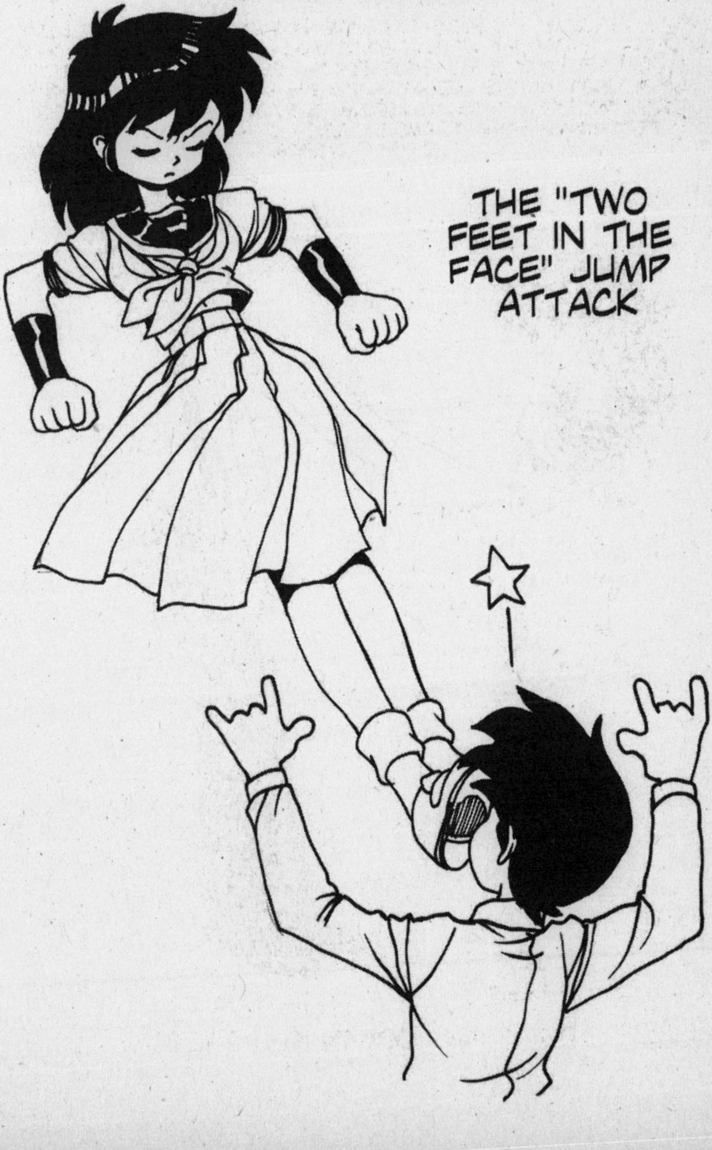
THE "TWO FEET IN THE FACE" JUMP ATTACK

HOW TO DRAW MANGA

BODY LANGUAGE
FIGHT SCENES

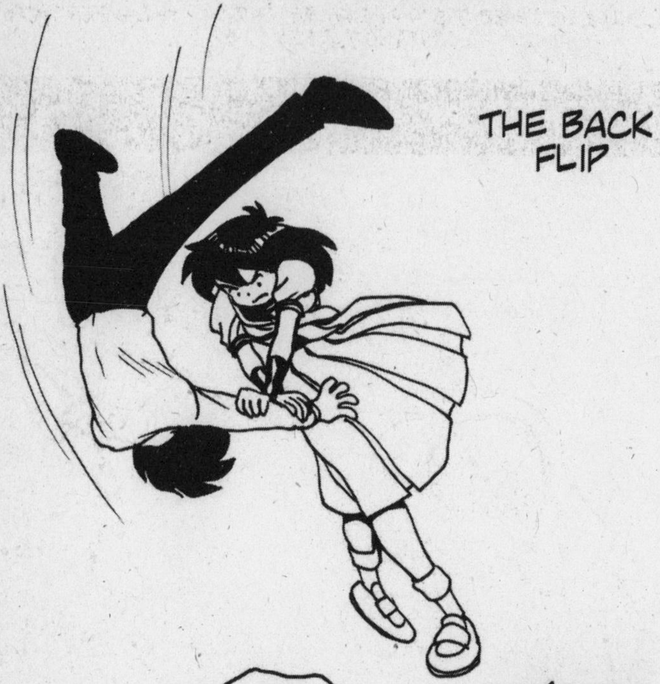
THE BACK FLIP

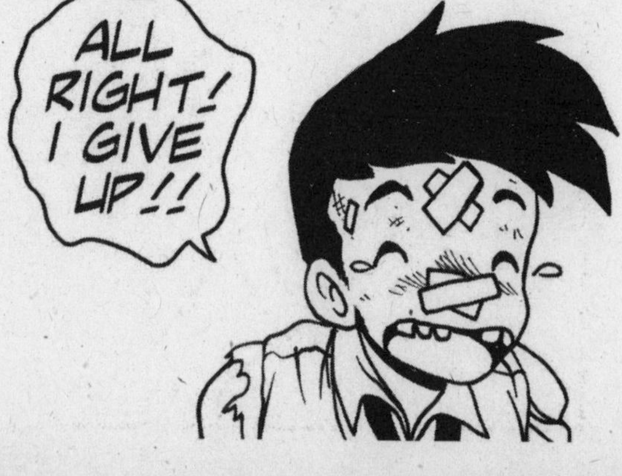
ALL RIGHT! I GIVE UP!!

HOW TO DRAW MANGA

BODY LANGUAGE
FIGHT SCENES

OF COURSE, NOT EVERYONE IS AS EASY AS LENDO. A TYPICAL FIGHT SCENE
CONTAINS THE FOUR "C"S.

① CONFRONTATION

HOW TO DRAW MANGA

BODY LANGUAGE
FIGHT SCENES

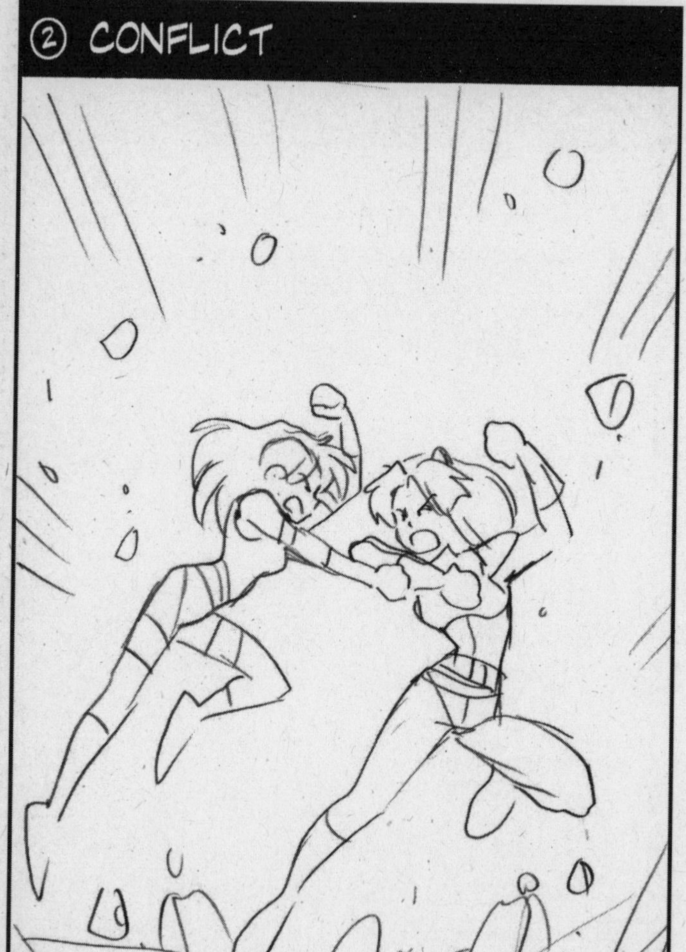
② CONFLICT

HOW TO DRAW MANGA

BODY LANGUAGE
FIGHT SCENES

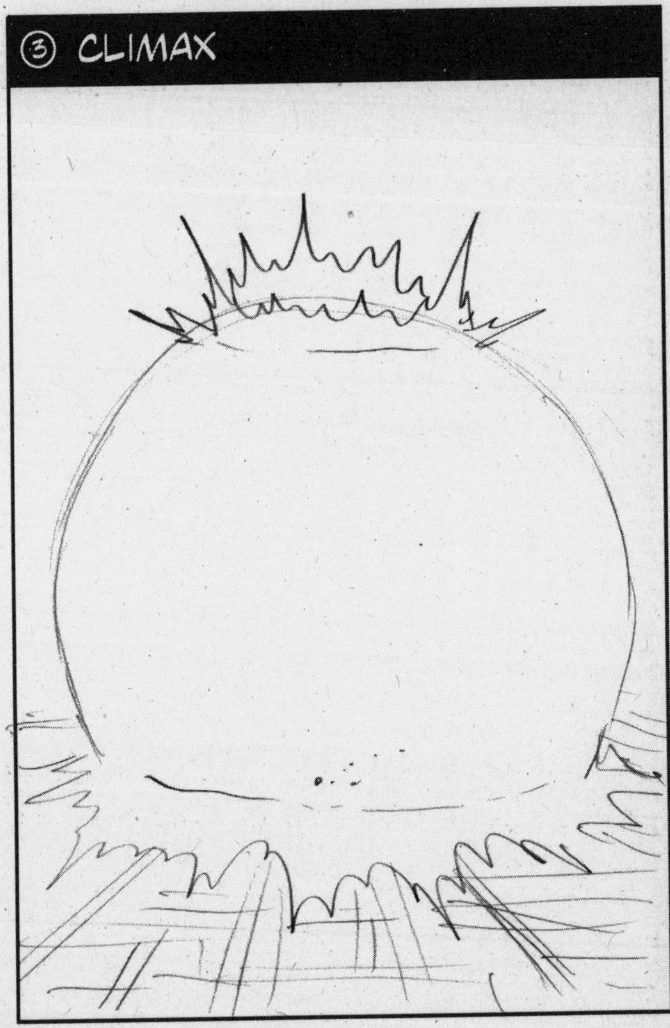
③ CLIMAX

HOW TO DRAW MANGA

BODY LANGUAGE
FIGHT SCENES

④ CONCLUSION

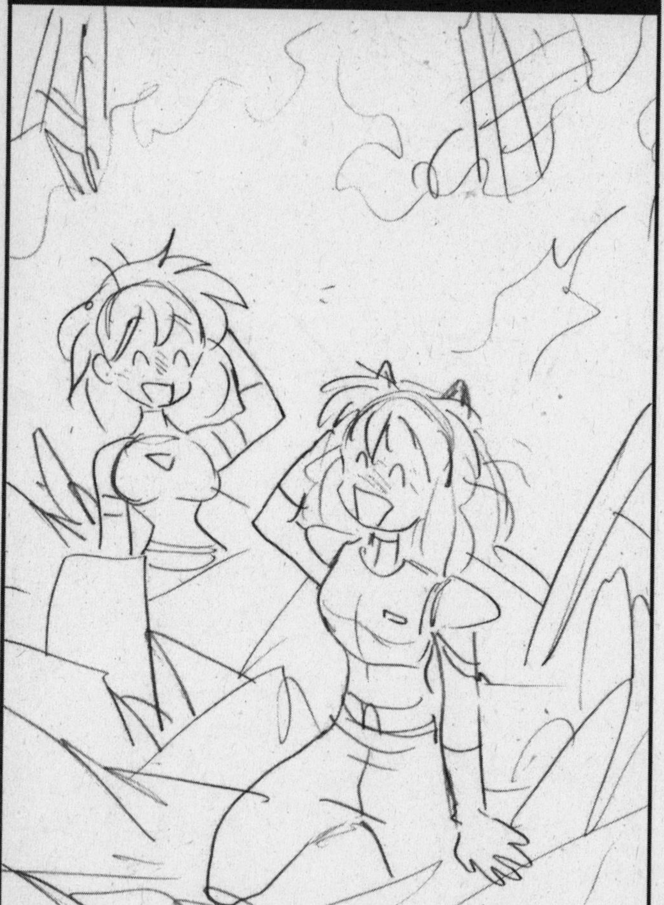

BODY LANGUAGE

HERE ARE SOME OTHER ACTIONS THAT YOU MIGHT FIND USEFUL.

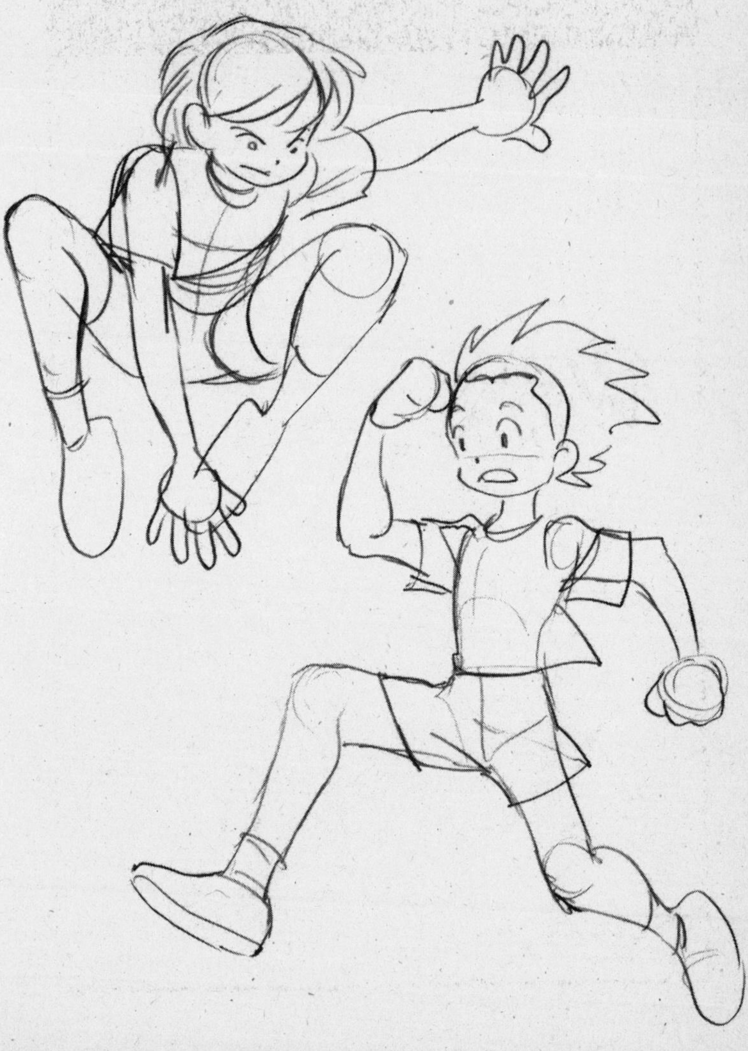

HOW TO DRAW MANGA

BODY LANGUAGE

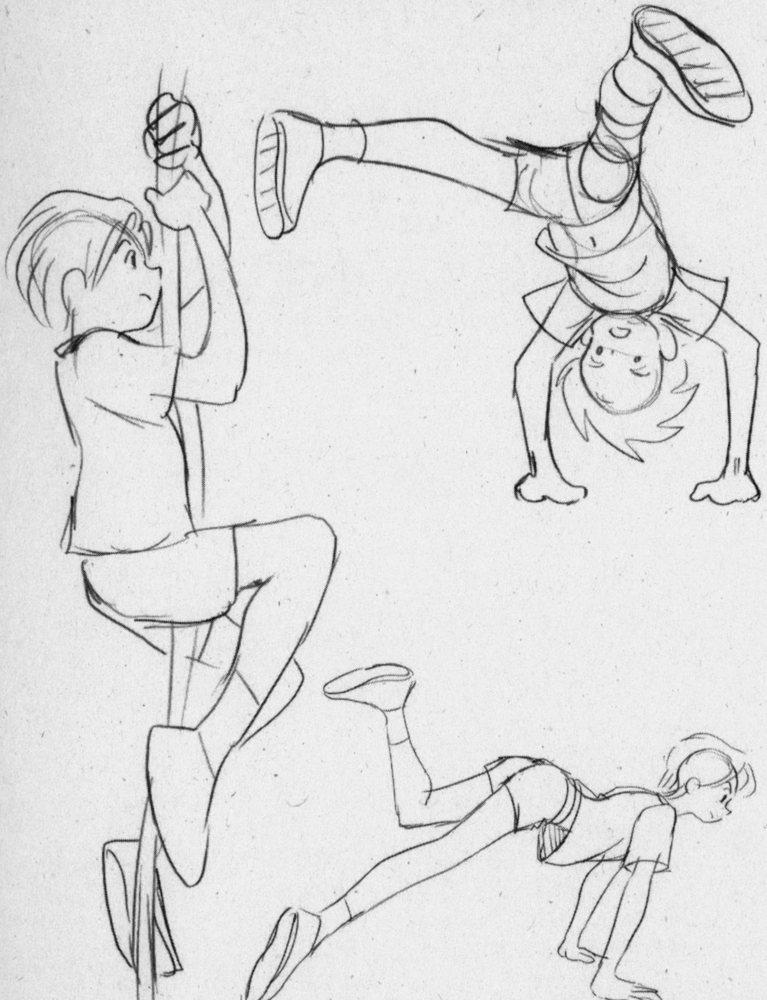

PRACTICE PAGE

HOW TO DRAW MANGA

BODY LANGUAGE
FIGHT SCENES

THE FACE IS THE FOCUS OF ATTENTION ON THE HUMAN BODY. IT CAN SAY SO MUCH WITHOUT SAYING ANYTHING AT ALL. HERE ARE SOME STANDARD EXPRESSIONS I USE IN NHS...

VERY HAPPY OR EXCITED

HAPPY OR PLEASED

WILY

CACKLING

HOW TO DRAW MANGA

BODY LANGUAGE
EXPRESSIONS

APOLOGETIC

ANGRY
SHOUTING

SAD

SURPRISE OR
SHOCK

HOW TO DRAW MANGA

BODY LANGUAGE
EXPRESSIONS

ANGRY
GRITTING

MODEST

BORED

SNOTTY

YOU CAN MIX AND MATCH EMOTIONS TO CONVEY A CERTAIN
LOOK TO EACH CHARACTER.

HOW TO DRAW MANGA

BODY TYPES
MALE BODY TYPE

SUPERHEROES AND VILLAINS HAVE SEVERAL BODY TYPES. THE TYPE OF BODY ONE CHOOSES SAYS A GREAT DEAL ABOUT THE CHARACTER.

BODYBUILDER TYPE (AVERAGE)

A TYPICAL SUPERHERO OR VILLAIN BODY TYPE.

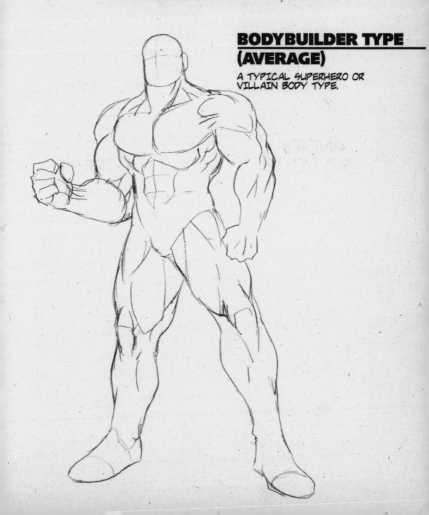

HOW TO DRAW MANGA

BODY TYPES

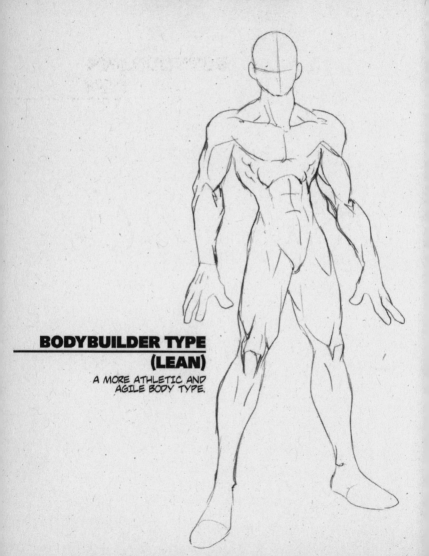

BODYBUILDER TYPE
(LEAN)
A MORE ATHLETIC AND
AGILE BODY TYPE.

HOW TO DRAW MANGA

BODY TYPES

BODYBUILDER
TYPE

HOW TO DRAW MANGA

BODY TYPES

SKINNY TEEN TYPE

NOTE:
THE THINNER THE NECK,
THE THINNER THE BODY.

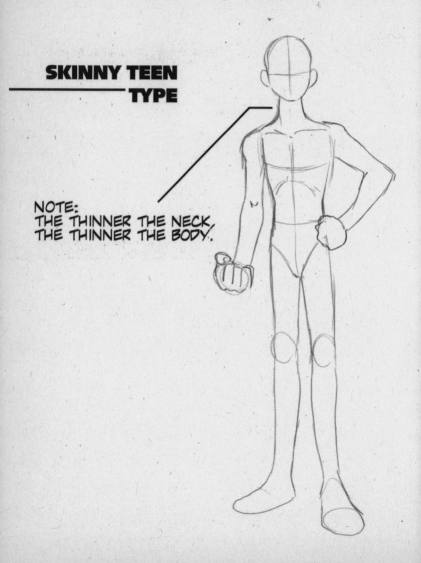

BODY TYPES

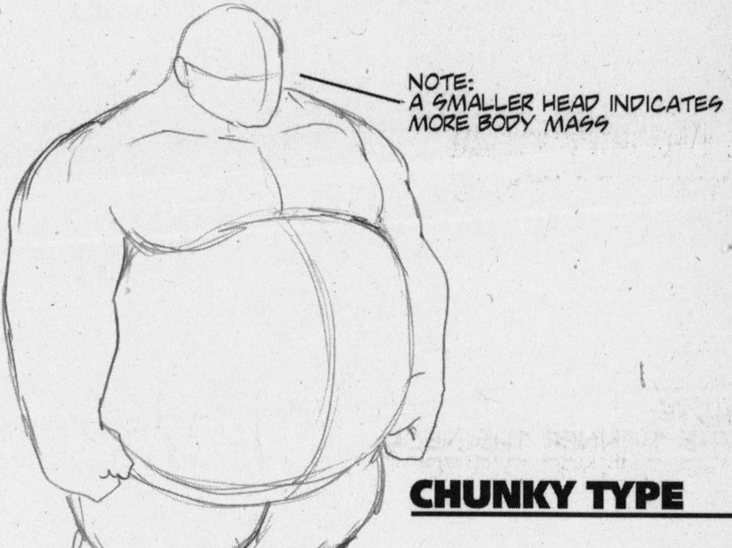
NOTE:
A SMALLER HEAD INDICATES
MORE BODY MASS

CHUNKY TYPE

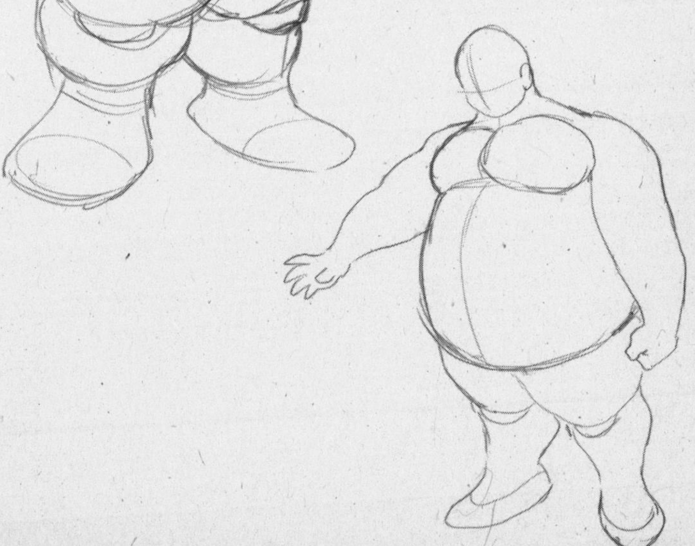

BODY TYPES

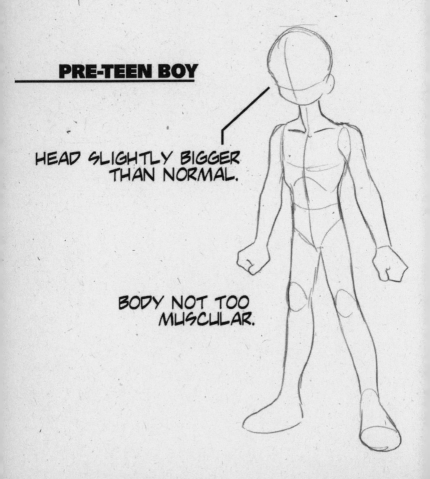

PRE-TEEN BOY

HEAD SLIGHTLY BIGGER
THAN NORMAL.

BODY NOT TOO
MUSCULAR.

BODY TYPES
THE HUSKY, MUSCULAR MALE HERO/VILLAIN

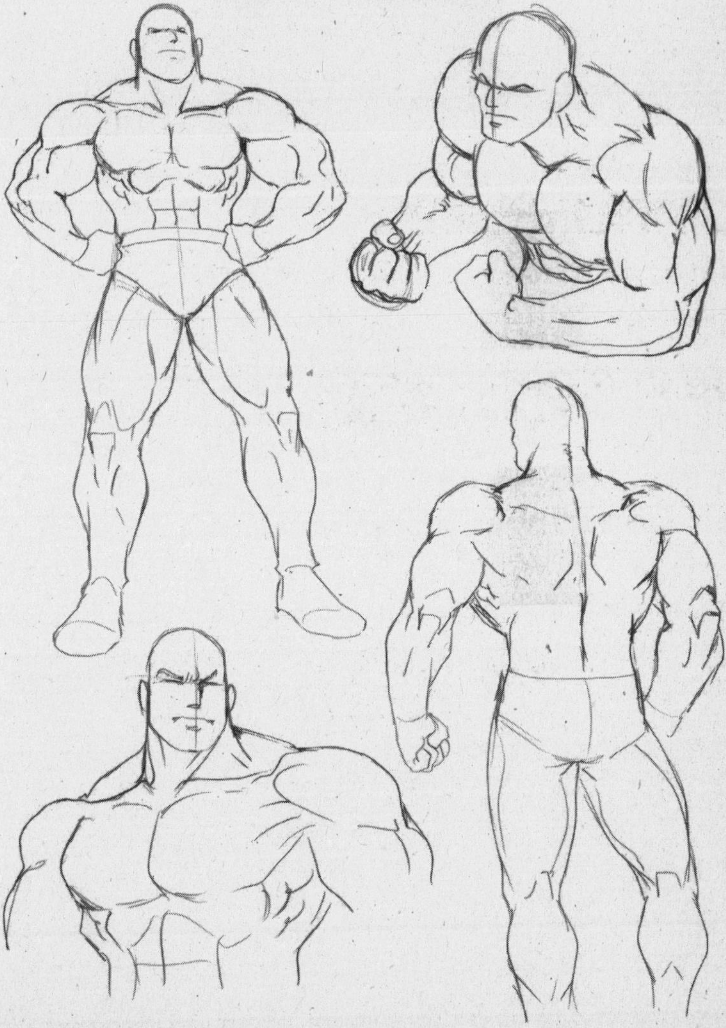

HOW TO DRAW MANGA

BODY TYPES

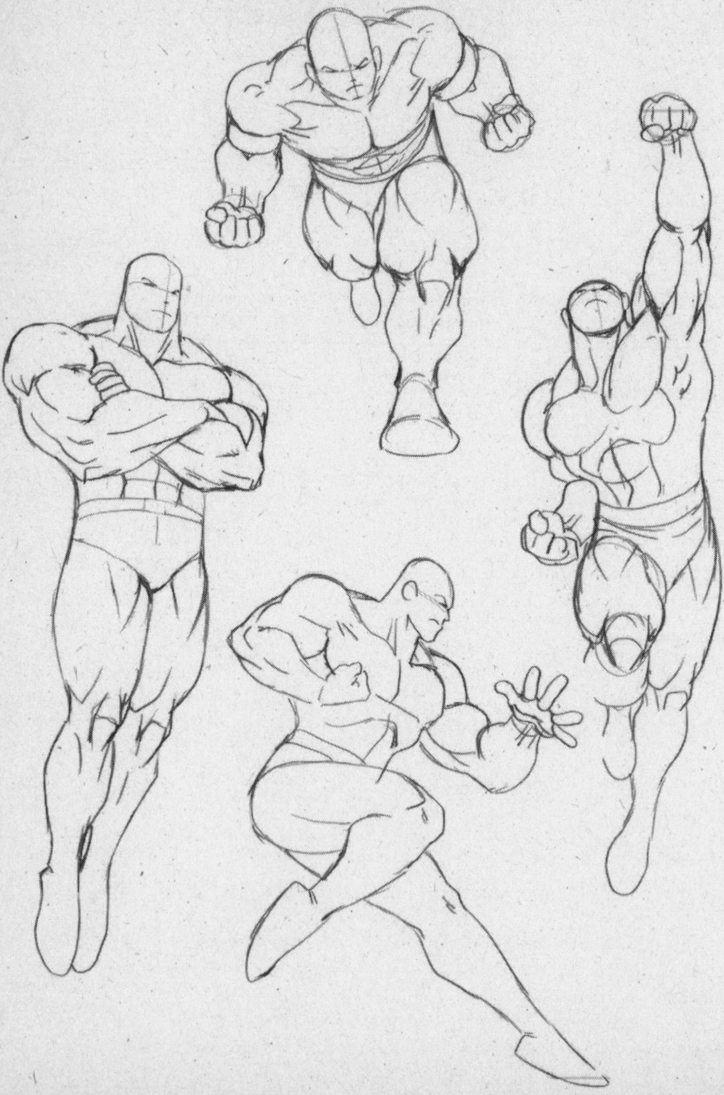

HOW TO DRAW MANGA

BODY TYPES
FEMALE BODY TYPE
FEMALES TEND TO BE LESS MUSCULAR AND
MORE CURVEY TO HEIGHTEN THEIR FEMININITY.

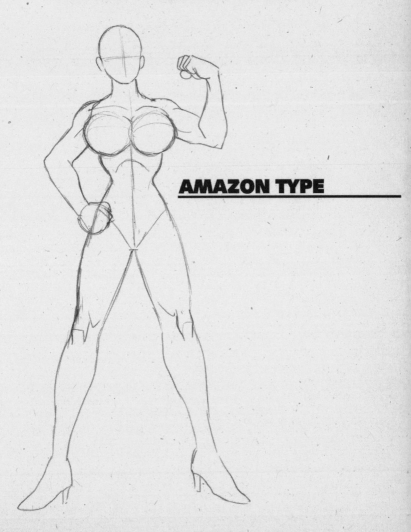

AMAZON TYPE

HOW TO DRAW MANGA

BODY TYPES

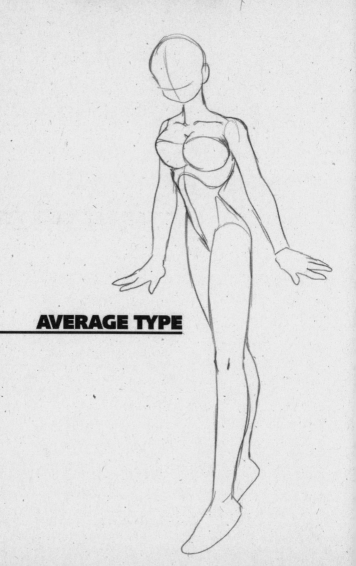

AVERAGE TYPE

BODY TYPES

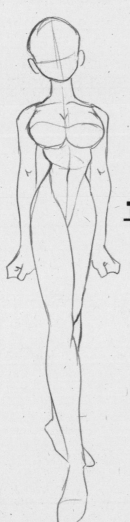

TEENAGE GIRL TYPE

BODY TYPES

PRE-TEEN GIRL TYPE

HOW TO DRAW MANGA

BODY TYPES

THE **HEROIC FEMALE**

OR **EVIL VILLAINESS**

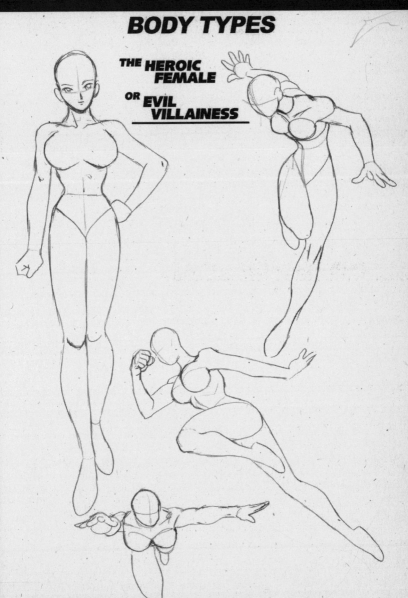

PRACTICE PAGE

CAPES!

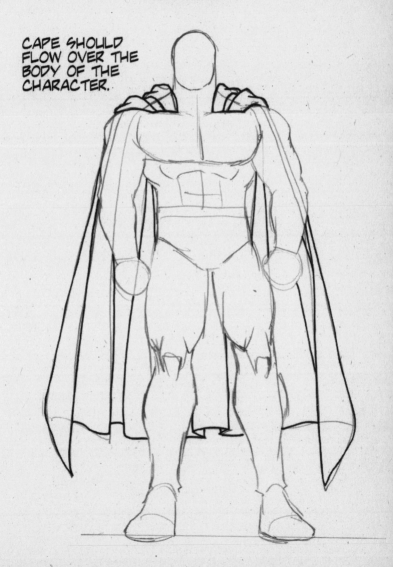

CAPE SHOULD
FLOW OVER THE
BODY OF THE
CHARACTER.

HOW TO DRAW MANGA

CAPES!

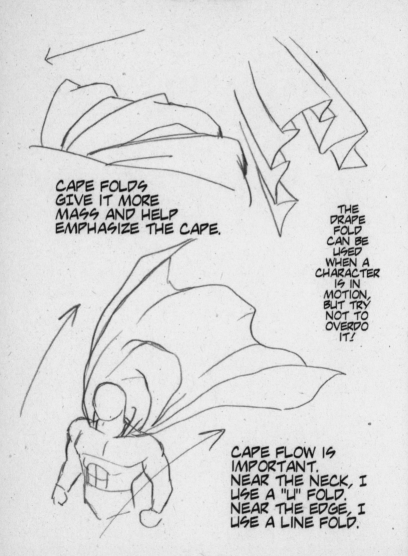

CAPE FOLDS GIVE IT MORE MASS AND HELP EMPHASIZE THE CAPE.

THE DRAPE FOLD CAN BE USED WHEN A CHARACTER IS IN MOTION, BUT TRY NOT TO OVERDO IT!

CAPE FLOW IS IMPORTANT. NEAR THE NECK, I USE A "U" FOLD. NEAR THE EDGE, I USE A LINE FOLD.

HOW TO DRAW MANGA

CAPES!

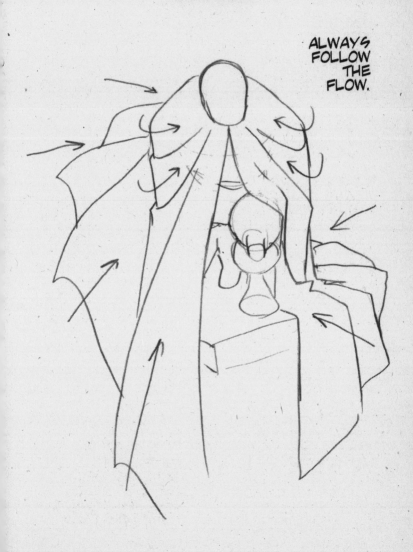

ALWAYS FOLLOW THE FLOW.

HOW TO DRAW MANGA

CAPES!

FOLDS ARE VERY
IMPORTANT FOR GIVING
THE CAPE MOVEMENT
AND DRAMA.

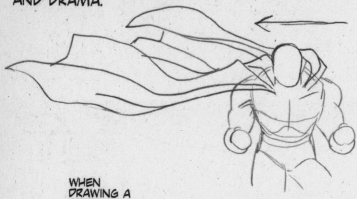

WHEN
DRAWING A
CAPE, FOLLOW
THE FLOW
OF THE
BODY.

CAPES!

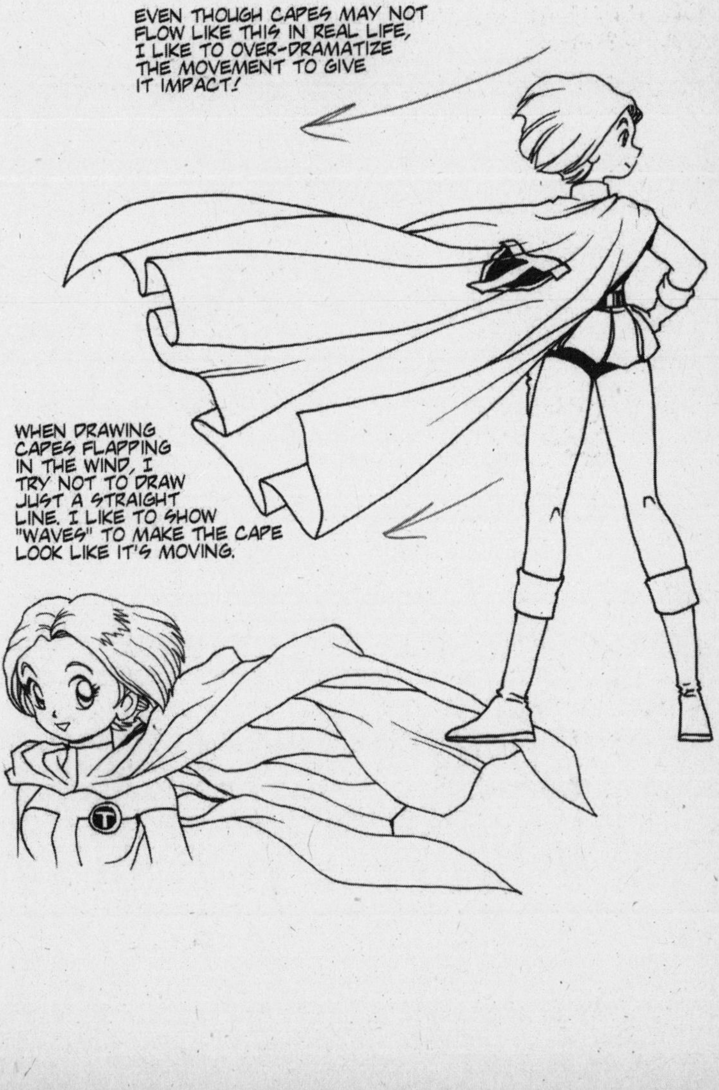
EVEN THOUGH CAPES MAY NOT FLOW LIKE THIS IN REAL LIFE, I LIKE TO OVER-DRAMATIZE THE MOVEMENT TO GIVE IT IMPACT!
WHEN DRAWING CAPES FLAPPING IN THE WIND, I TRY NOT TO DRAW JUST A STRAIGHT LINE. I LIKE TO SHOW "WAVES" TO MAKE THE CAPE LOOK LIKE IT'S MOVING.
T

HOW TO DRAW MANGA

CAPES!

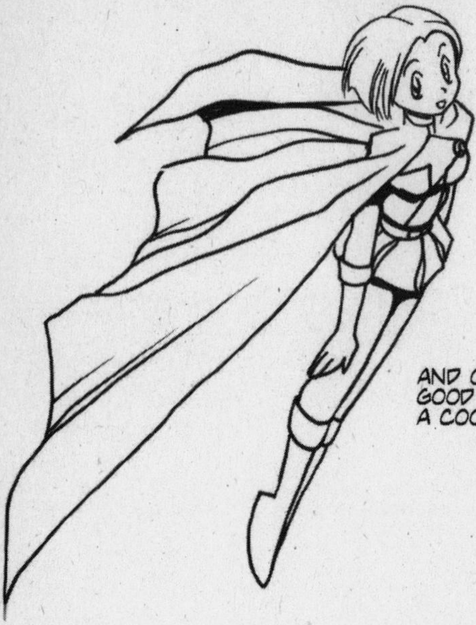

AND OF COURSE, WHAT WOULD A GOOD SUPERHERO BE WITHOUT A COOL FLYING POSE!

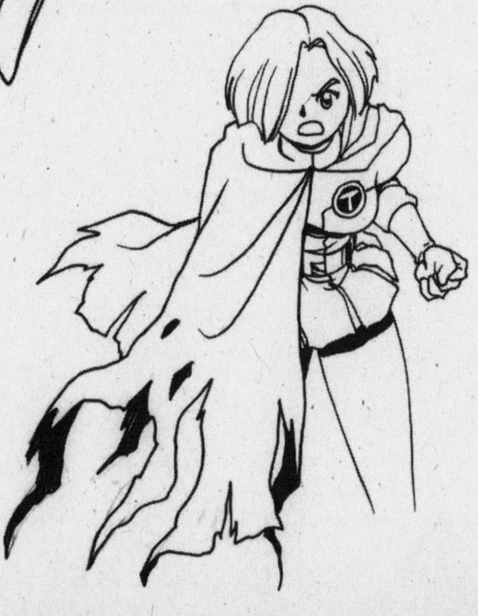

TORN OR FRAYED CAPES LOOK MORE TATTERED IF YOU GIVE THEM JAGGED EDGES!

PRACTICE PAGE

HOW TO DRAW MANGA

DRAW ICHI KUN

ONE OF THE MORE POPULAR CHARACTERS IN NINJA HIGH SCHOOL IS THE NINJA FEMME FATALE, ICHI KUN ICHINOHEI. ORIGINALLY CALLED ITCHY KOO, SHE HAS PROVEN TO BE ONE OF THE MORE INTERESTING CHARACTERS TO DRAW.

IF YOU HAVE SOME OF THE EARLIER EDITIONS OF HOW TO DRAW MANGA, YOU'VE LEARNED THE BASIC BODY TYPES AND HOW TO CONSTRUCT THEM.

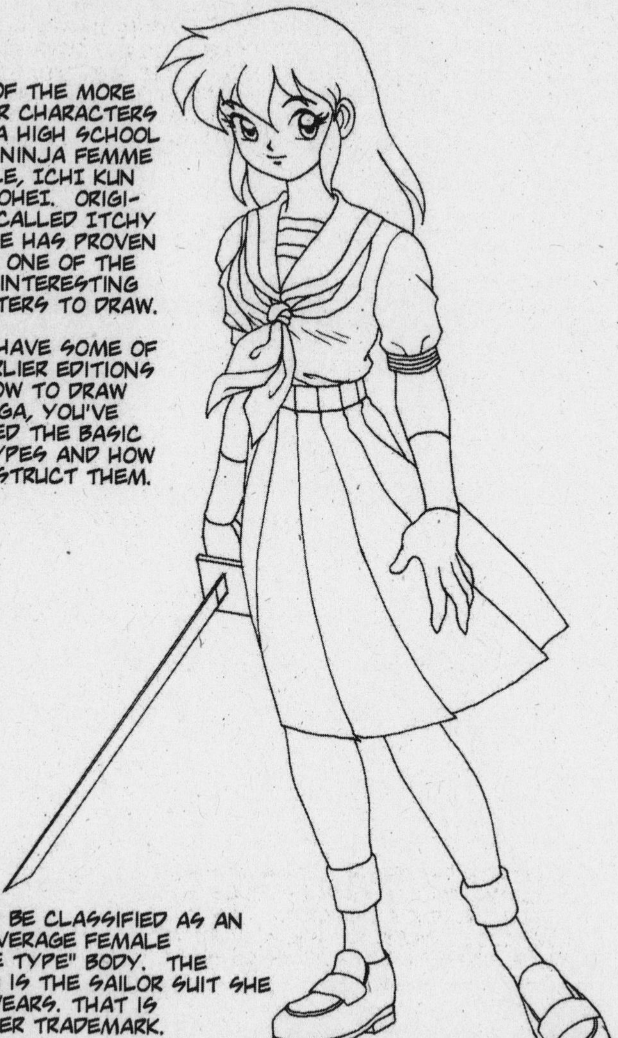

ICHI CAN BE CLASSIFIED AS AN "AVERAGE FEMALE ANIME TYPE" BODY. THE MAIN THING IS THE SAILOR SUIT SHE WEARS. THAT IS HER TRADEMARK.

HOW TO DRAW MANGA

DRAW ICHI KUN

ICHI'S NINJA OUTFIT IS NOT THE
TRADITIONAL LOOSE GARB OF A
NINJA, BUT A SKINTIGHT NUMBER
WITH FLOWING SASHES. NOT
EXACTLY REGULATION NINJA
CLOTHING, BUT THEN, SHE ISN'T AN
ORDINARY NINJA.

ICHI'S SISTER, HITOMI, WEARS A
LONG SKIRT, DARK NAVY BLUE IN
COLOR, FOR A UNIFORM. THIS IS
ACTUALLY MORE IN LINE WITH WHAT
REAL JAPANESE SCHOOLGIRLS WEAR.

DRAW ICHI KUN

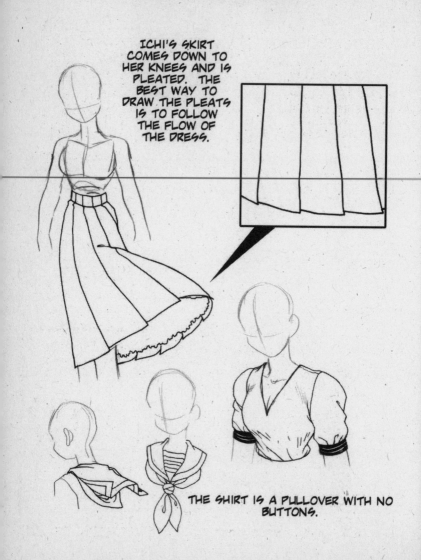

ICHI'S SKIRT COMES DOWN TO HER KNEES AND IS PLEATED. THE BEST WAY TO DRAW THE PLEATS IS TO FOLLOW THE FLOW OF THE DRESS.

THE SHIRT IS A PULLOVER WITH NO BUTTONS.

DRAW ICHI KUN

ICHI'S NINJA SWORD. THE TOTAL LENGTH IS ABOUT THE LENGTH OF HER ARM.

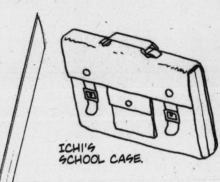

ICHI'S SCHOOL CASE.

ICHI'S REGULATION SCHOOL SHOES.

HOW TO DRAW MANGA

DRAW ICHI KUN

1

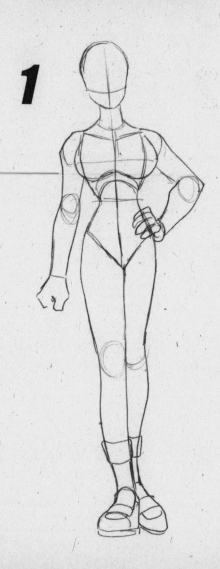

HOW TO DRAW MANGA

DRAW ICHI KUN

2

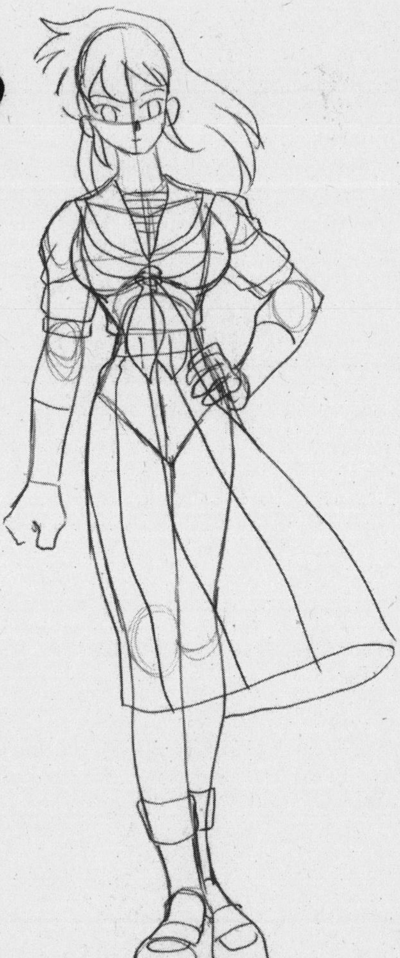

DRAW ICHI KUN

3

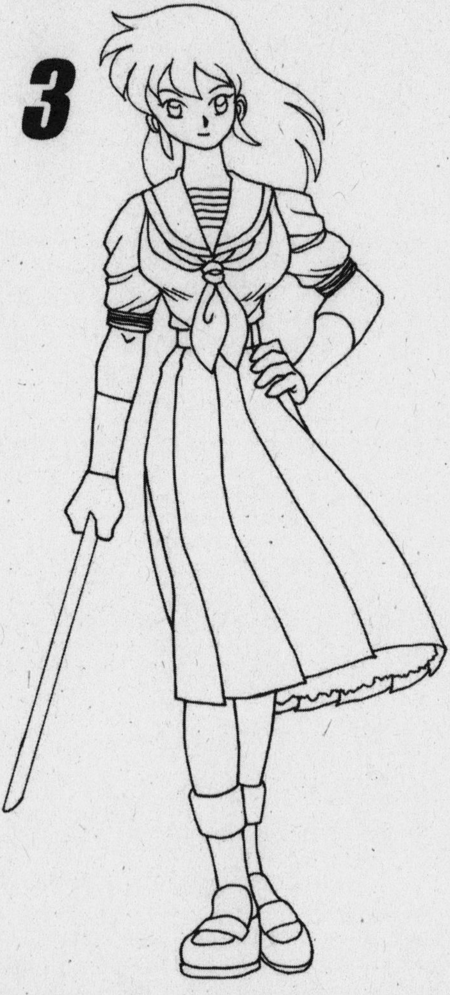

PRACTICE PAGE

HOW TO DRAW MANGA

DRAW ICHI KUN

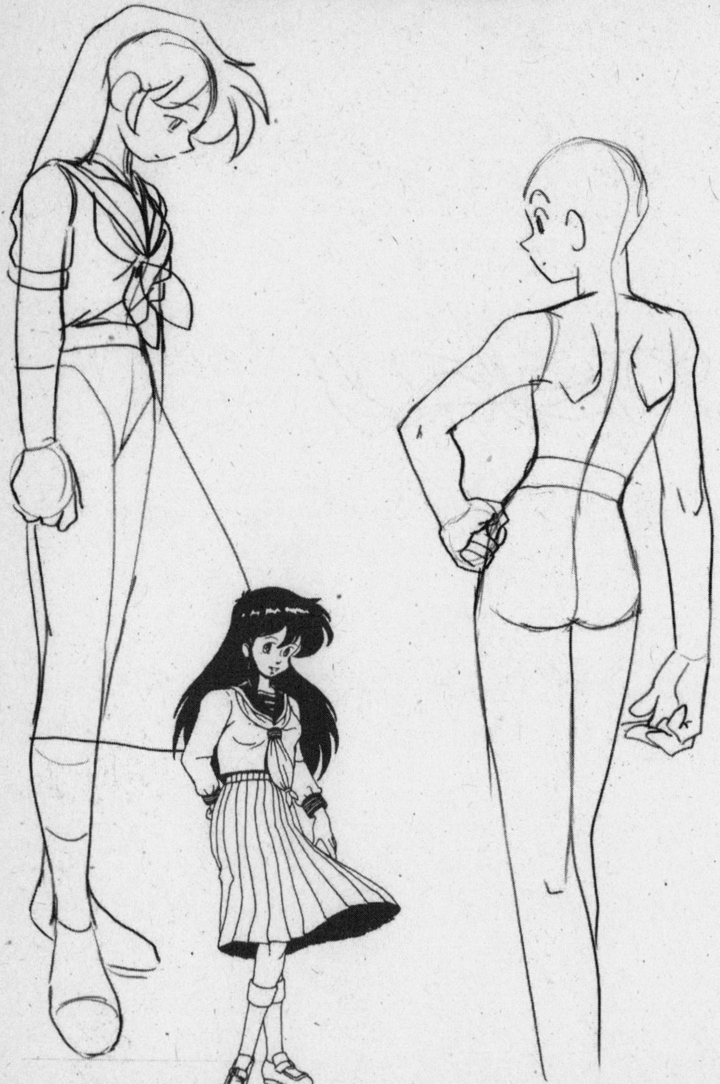

HOW TO DRAW MANGA

DRAW ICHI KUN

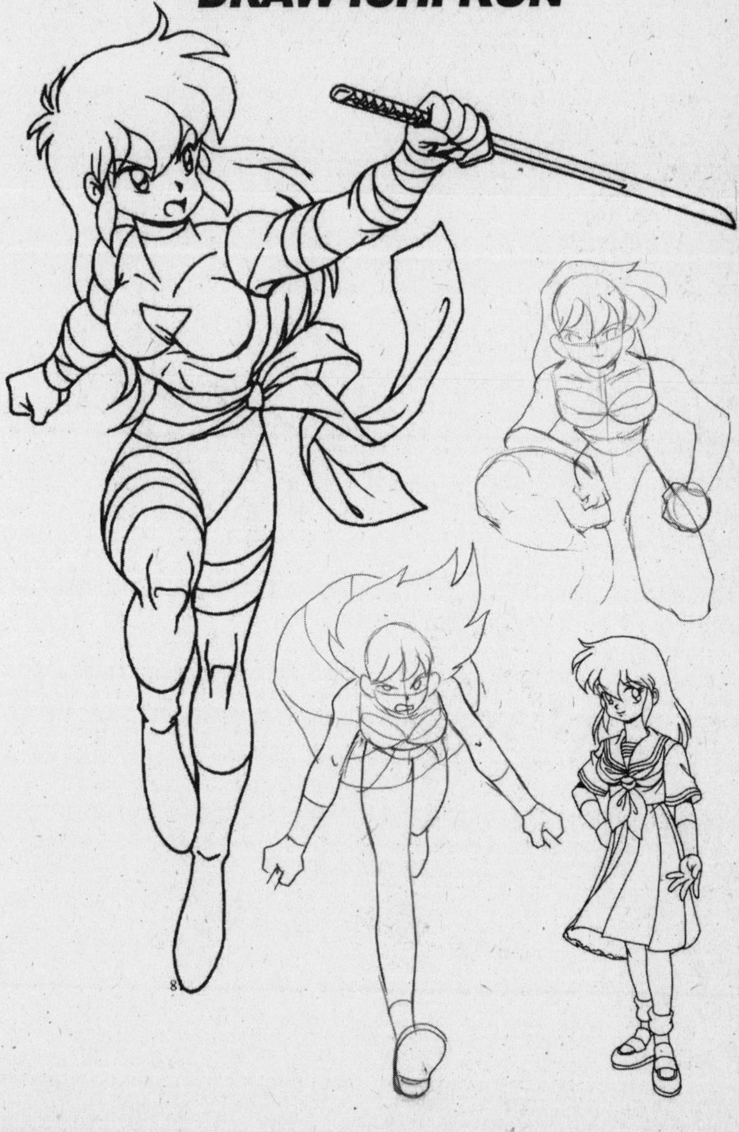

HOW TO DRAW MANGA

DRAW ICHI KUN

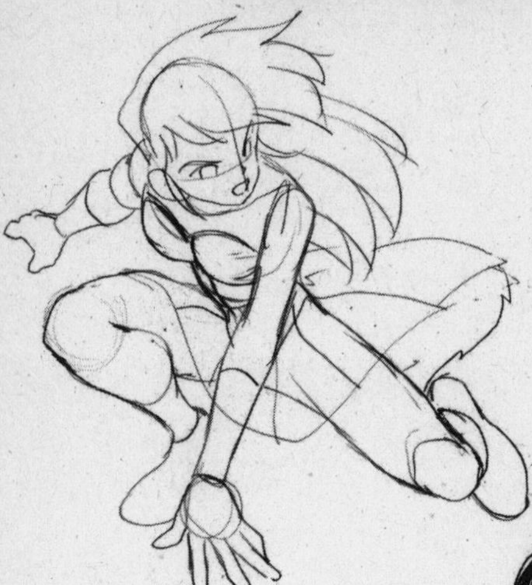

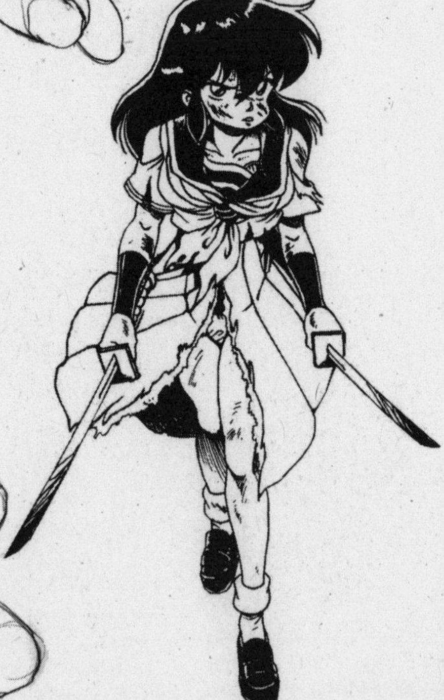

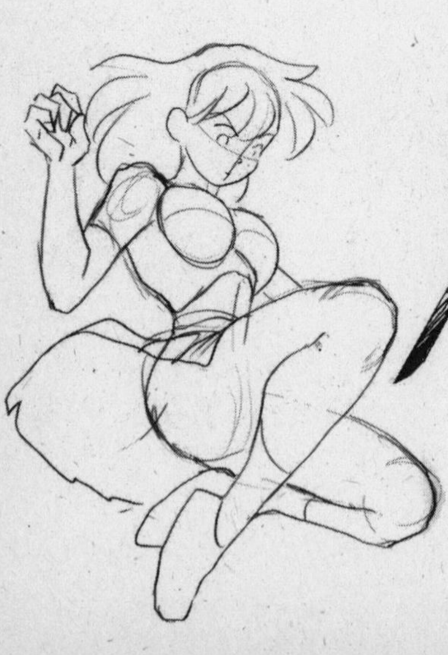

HOW TO DRAW MANGA

DRAW ICHI KUN

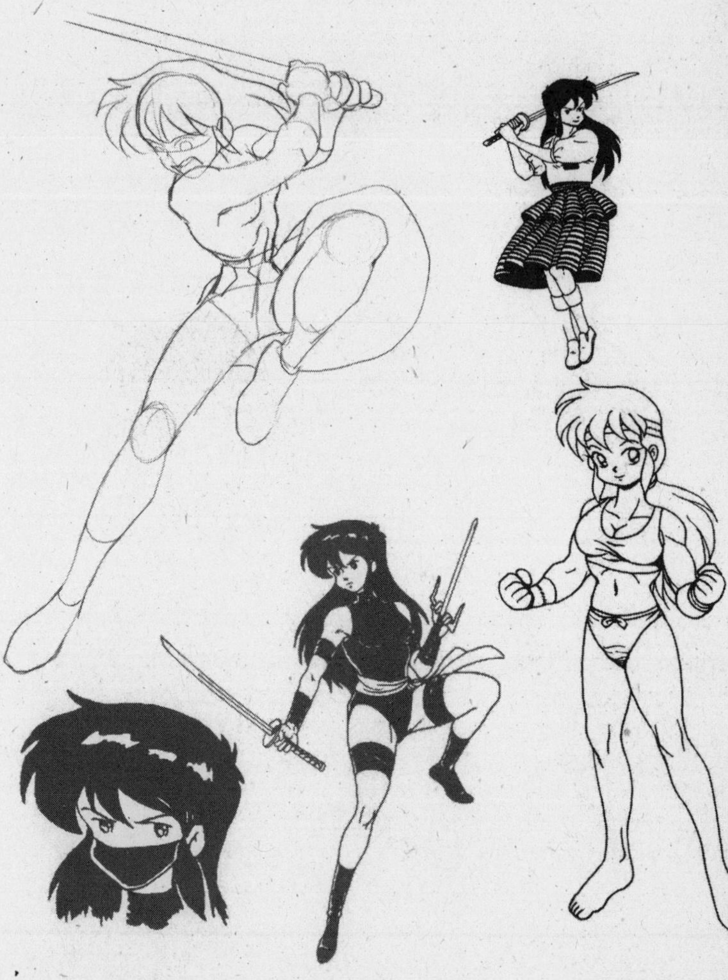

HOW TO DRAW MANGA

SMALL-BODIED TYPES

ONE OF THE MORE BIZARRE ASPECTS OF MANGA IS THE DRAWING STYLE KNOWN AS "SD" OR "SUPER-DEFORMED." I CALL IT "SMALL-BODIED," THOUGH IT IS ALSO CALLED "CHIBI." THIS IS USUALLY EMPLOYED TO CREATE AN INCREDIBLY CUTE CHARACTER OR TO MAKE A NORMAL CHARACTER LOOK LIKE IT HAS INHABITED A CHILD'S BODY. I CAN'T EXPLAIN IT, BUT IT IS A MAINSTAY OF MANGA AND I FIND IT STRANGELY APPEALING FROM AN ARTISTIC VIEWPOINT. HERE I WILL TRY TO SHOW HOW I HANDLE THESE IMPISH CHARACTERS.

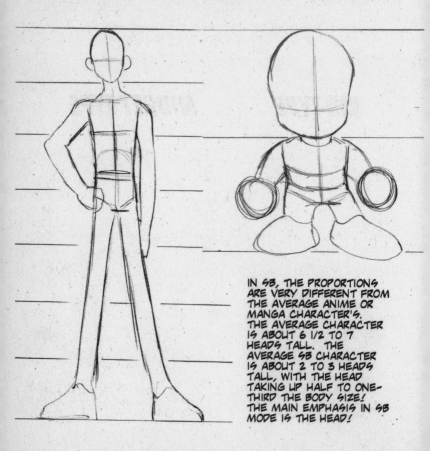

IN SB, THE PROPORTIONS ARE VERY DIFFERENT FROM THE AVERAGE ANIME OR MANGA CHARACTER'S. THE AVERAGE CHARACTER IS ABOUT 6 1/2 TO 7 HEADS TALL. THE AVERAGE SB CHARACTER IS ABOUT 2 TO 3 HEADS TALL, WITH THE HEAD TAKING UP HALF TO ONE-THIRD THE BODY SIZE! THE MAIN EMPHASIS IN SB MODE IS THE HEAD!

SMALL-BODIED TYPES

SURPRISINGLY ENOUGH, THERE ARE RULES TO DRAWING EVEN IN SB MODE. EVEN THE RULES OF ANATOMY AND PROPORTION ARE IMPORTANT, AS WELL AS THE USUAL RULES OF PERSPECTIVE. IT IS NOT ENOUGH JUST TO DRAW SUPER-CUTE CHARACTERS. THEY STILL NEED TO INTERACT AND MOVE LIKE REAL CHARACTERS. IF THIS WERE A PEANUTS STRIP, YOU COULD GET AWAY WITH SB ON A LIMITED BASIS, BUT THIS IS MANGA! AND WE DO THINGS DIFFERENTLY HERE!

THERE ARE SEVERAL BODY TYPES I USE WHEN I DRAW IN SB MODE:

KID TYPE

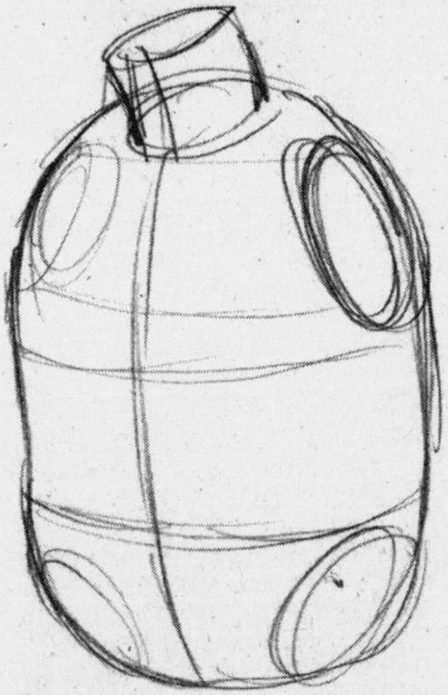

KIND OF CHUNKY AND SQUAT. I USUALLY USE THIS TO DRAW CHILDREN.

MIDGET TYPE

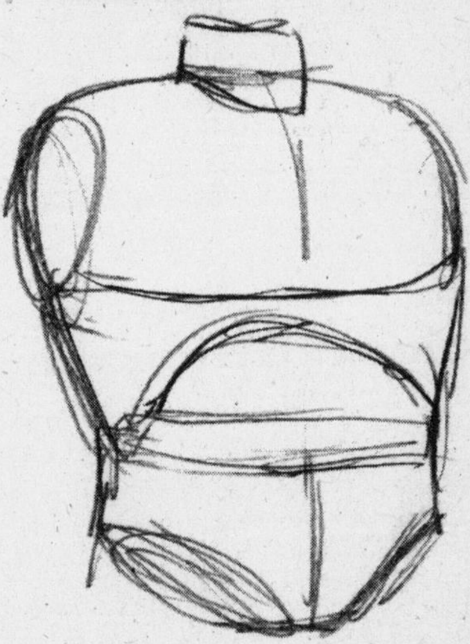

I USE THIS TYPE TO SHOW ADULT CHARACTERS IN CUTE BODIES.

SMALL-BODIED TYPES

THIN TYPE

CHIBI TYPE

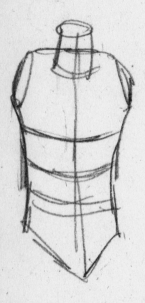

WHEN I WANT TO SHOW TEENS, I USUALLY USE THIS TYPE.

CHIBI TYPE IS USED AS A SORT OF GENERIC, CATCH-ALL TYPE OF BODY. I USUALLY USE THIS WHEN I NEED AN SB CHARACTER QUICKLY.

SMALL-BODIED TYPES
HANDS AND ARMS

DOING ARMS AND HANDS IS VERY SIMPLE IF
YOU REMEMBER ONE BASIC RULE: CIRCLES!
USING CIRCLES, YOU CAN CREATE ALMOST
ANY HAND POSITION AND MAKE YOUR SB
CHARACTER MORE DYNAMIC.

TUBE   SECTIONED

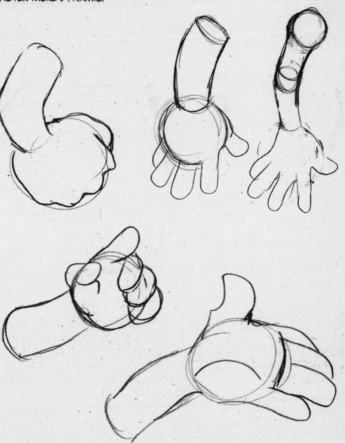

SMALL-BODIED TYPES
HANDS AND ARMS

FOR FINGERS, I IMAGINE LITTLE SAUSAGES AT THE END. FINGERNAILS ARE OPTIONAL. I USUALLY DRAW THE ARM IN SECTIONS. FOR THE REST, I USE THE TUBE-TYPE ARM.

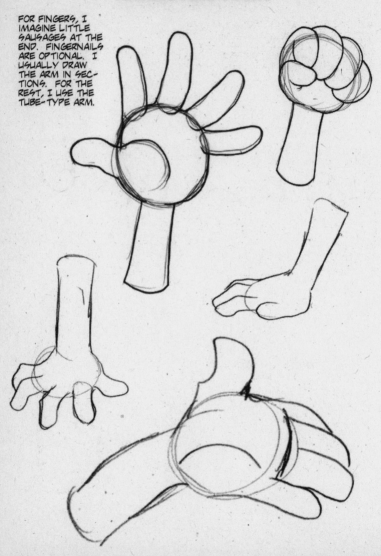

HOW TO DRAW MANGA

SMALL-BODIED TYPES
LEGS AND FEET

SIMILARLY TO ARMS AND HANDS, THE
MAIN THING TO REMEMBER ABOUT FEET IS
OVALS. YOU CAN DRAW THE FEET AND
TOES USING A SERIES OF OVALS. AGAIN,
WHEN I DRAW THE THIN TYPE OF BODY, I
USE SECTIONED LEGS AND FEET.

TUBE   SECTIONED

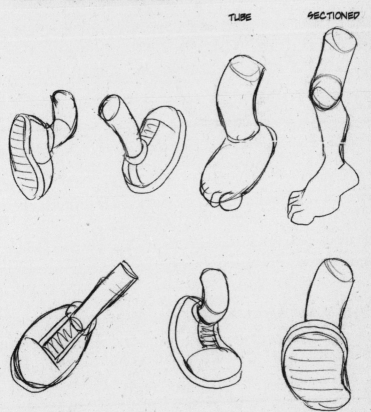

SMALL-BODIED TYPES

1: SKETCH A BASIC ROUGH OUTLINE STARTING WITH THE HEAD AND BODY TYPE.

SMALL-BODIED TYPES

2: SKETCH
IN THE ARMS
AND LEGS.

HOW TO DRAW MANGA

SMALL-BODIED TYPES

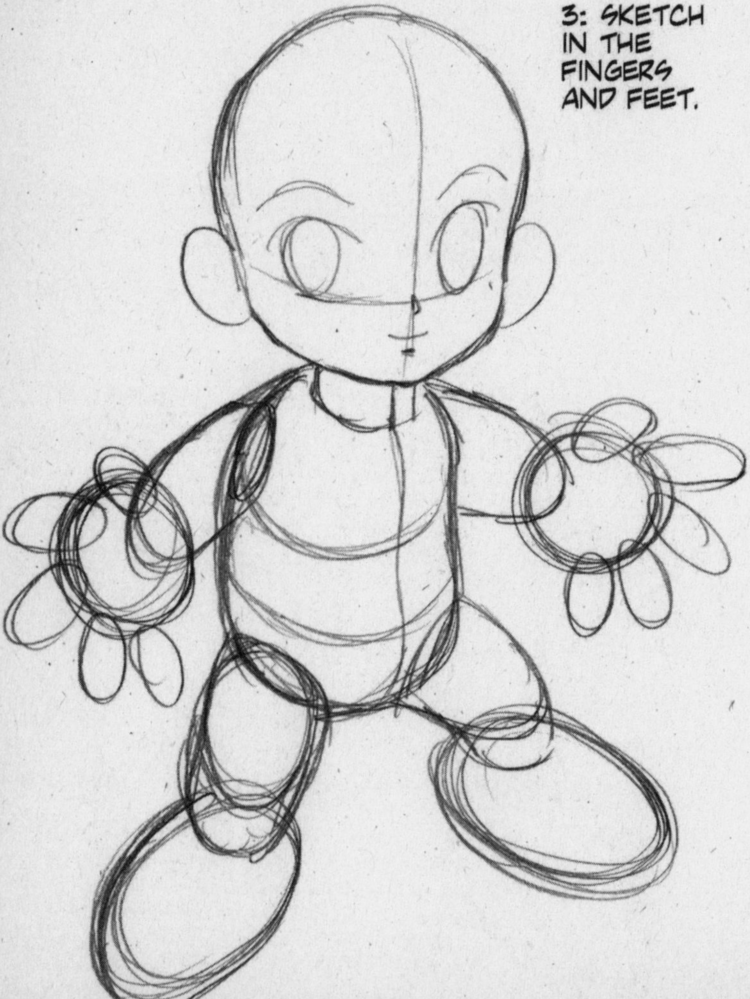
3: SKETCH
IN THE
FINGERS
AND FEET.

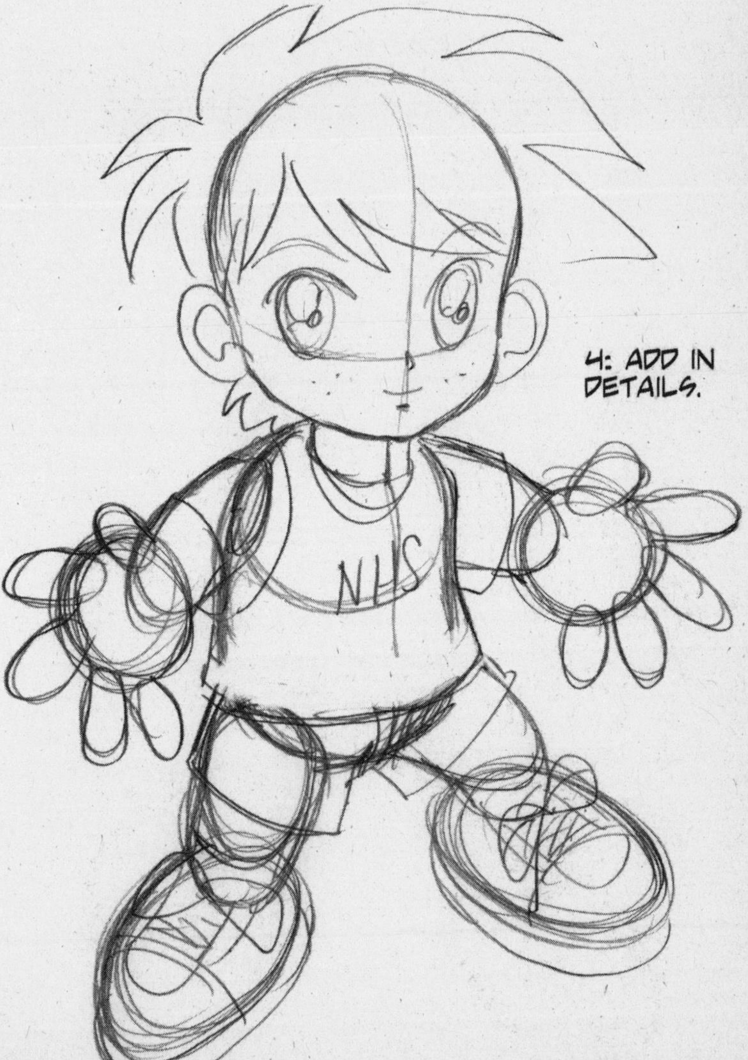
NHS
4: ADD IN DETAILS.

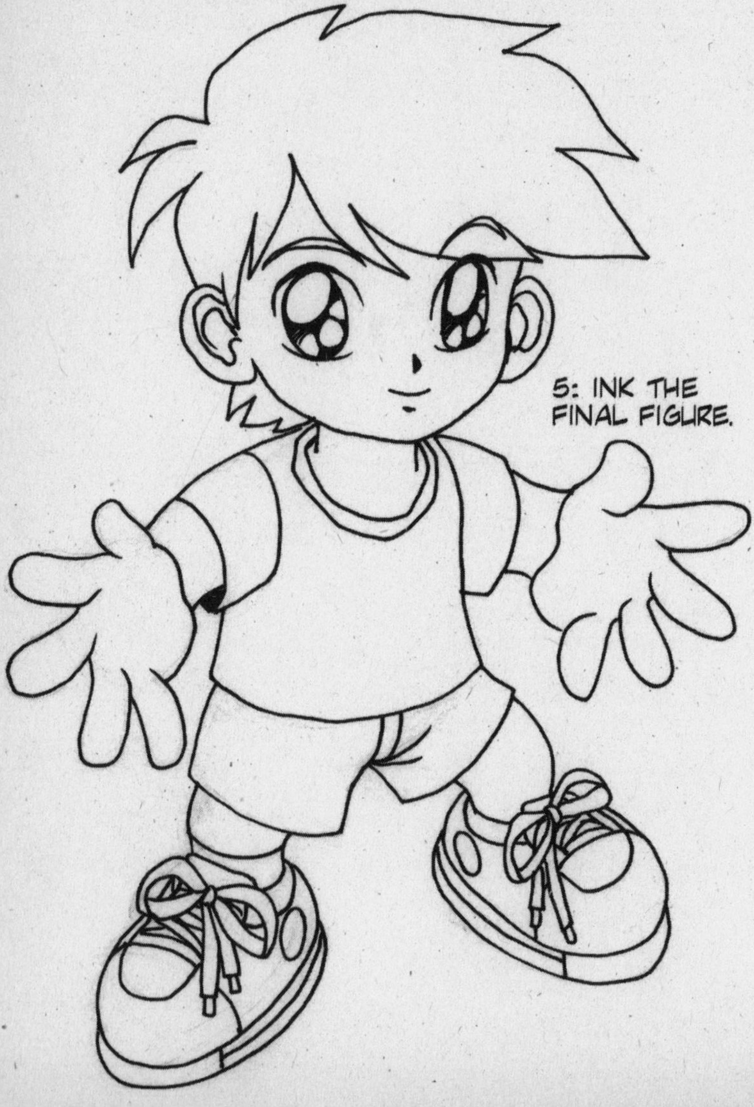

5: INK THE FINAL FIGURE.

PRACTICE PAGE

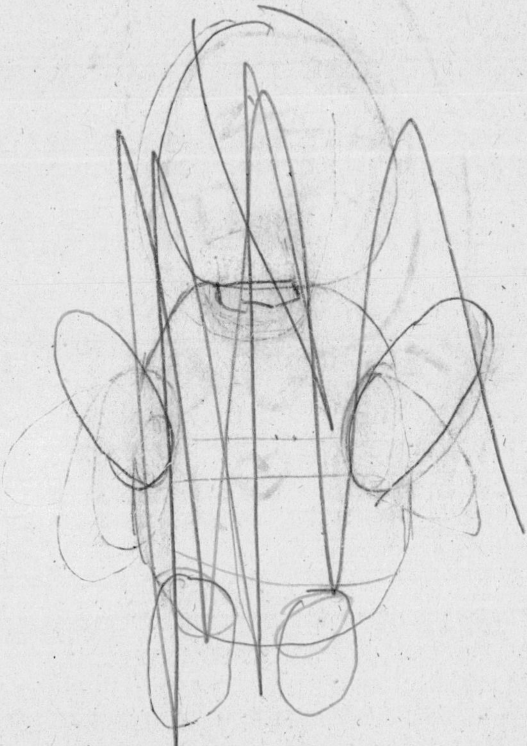

HOW TO DRAW MANGA

SMALL-BODIED TYPES

EXPRESSIONS

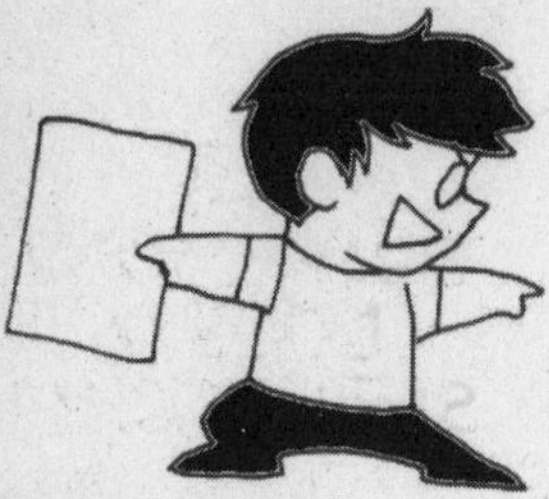

OKAY, ON TO THE NEXT LESSON!

I GOT SOME MORE VARIED EXPRESSIONS FOR YOU TO PORE OVER AND PRACTICE ON.

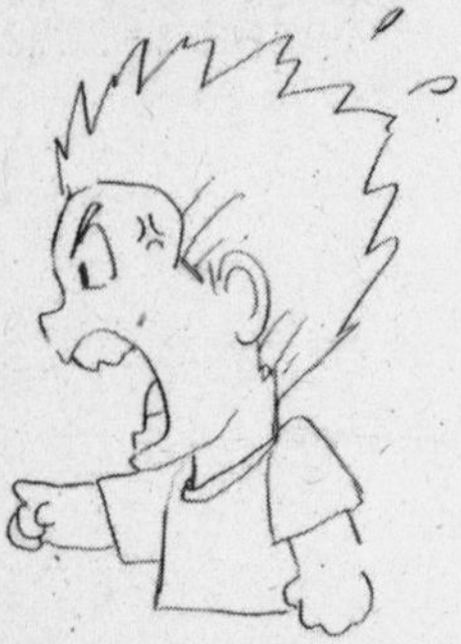

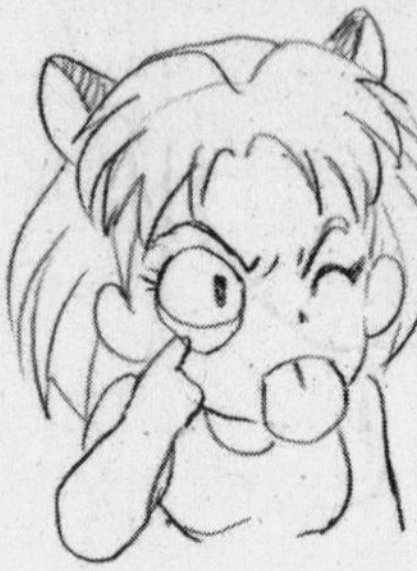

THERE ARE MORE EXPRESSIONS THAN THE USUAL BUG-EYED AND WIDE MOUTHED ONES. IN THE NEXT PAGES, I WILL SHOW YOU A NUMBEF OF THEM.

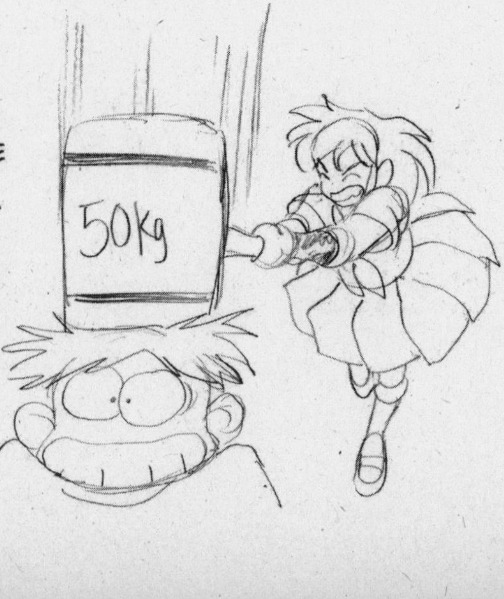
50Kg

HOW TO DRAW MANGA

SMALL-BODIED TYPES
EXPRESSIONS

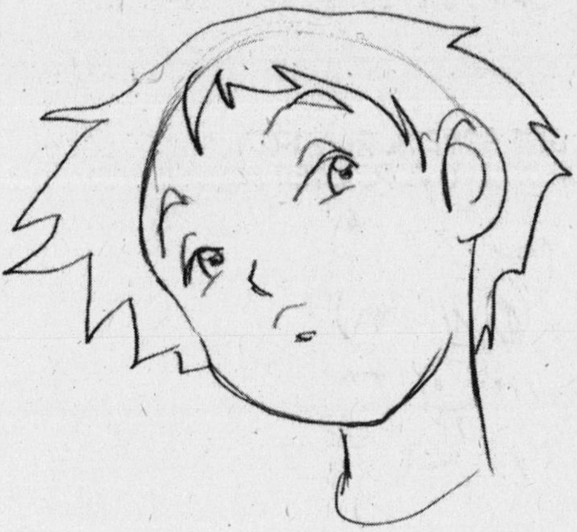

HMM...
SUSPICION?
DOUBT?
SKEPTICISM?

THIS EXPRESSION COVERS THOSE AND THEN SOME!

SLIGHTLY SCHEMING

A SMALL SMILE AND A DEVIOUS TURN OF THE EYES IS ALL IT TAKES

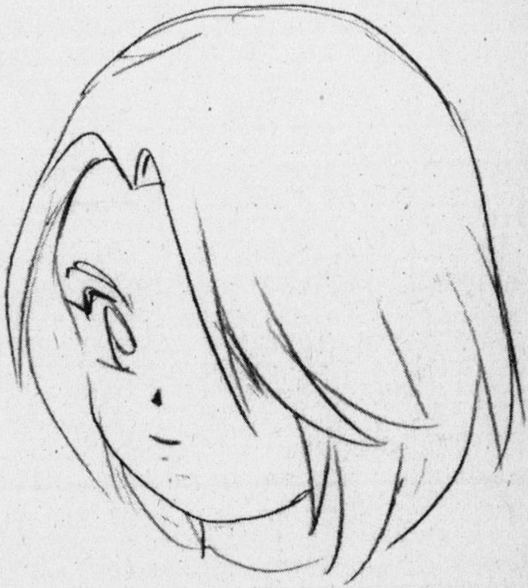

SMALL-BODIED TYPES
EXPRESSIONS

OVERWHELMING SURPRISE

THE CHIBI FIGURE HELPS A LOT

ON THE VERGE OF CRYING

SOMETIMES A HARD EXPRESSION TO DRAW.

SMALL-BODIED TYPES
EXPRESSIONS

SADNESS TO
THE POINT
OF CRYING
OR
SADLY
SYMPATHETIC.

BAWLING OUT!

(STREAMS OF
TEARS IS A
STANDARD
OF MANGA
STORYTELLING)

HOW TO DRAW MANGA

SMALL-BODIED TYPES
EXPRESSIONS

A GROWN MAN WEEPING LIKE A BABY IS AN UNUSUAL SOURCE OF HUMOR. SOMETIMES, THE UNEXPECTED IS A MOST EFFECTIVE WAY OF CONVEYING COMEDY.

ONCE AGAIN, THE RIVERS OF TEARS IS EMPLOYED TO EXAGGERATE THE EFFECT.

SNORING!

SURPRISE!!!

OR... KEPT AWAKE

HOW TO DRAW MANGA

SMALL-BODIED TYPES
EXPRESSIONS

UNEXPECTED
SURPRISE

OR

SUDDEN
EMBARASSMENT

ARGUMENTATIVE

LOUD REPLY

OR

SHOUTING A WARNING

SMALL-BODIED TYPES

EXPRESSIONS

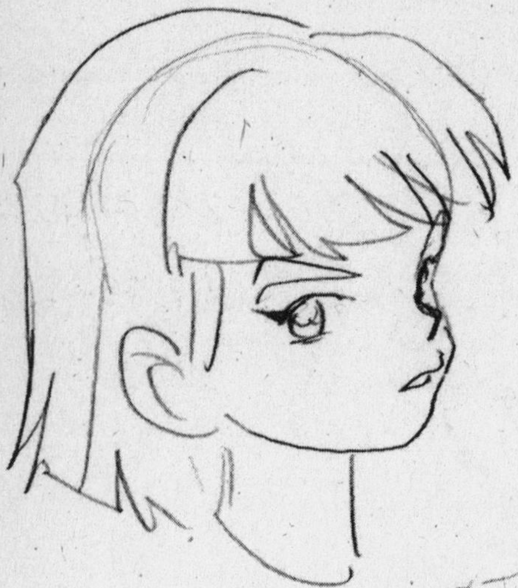

CONNIVING AND GOSSIPING

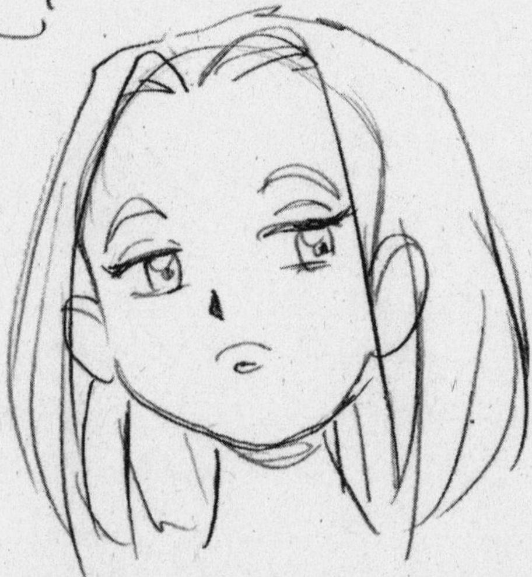

CONCEIT AND ARROGANCE

HOW TO DRAW MANGA

SMALL-BODIED TYPES
EXPRESSIONS

BASHFUL
SMILE
(AW GEE...)

WINK!

SMALL-BODIED TYPES
EXPRESSIONS

BURRRP!

HOT RETORT

HOW TO DRAW MANGA

SMALL-BODIED TYPES
EXPRESSIONS

"LOOK OUT
-- A WARNING"

SIMMERING ANGER

HAIR LOOKS FLAMELIKE

HOW TO DRAW MANGA

SMALL-BODIED TYPES
EXPRESSIONS

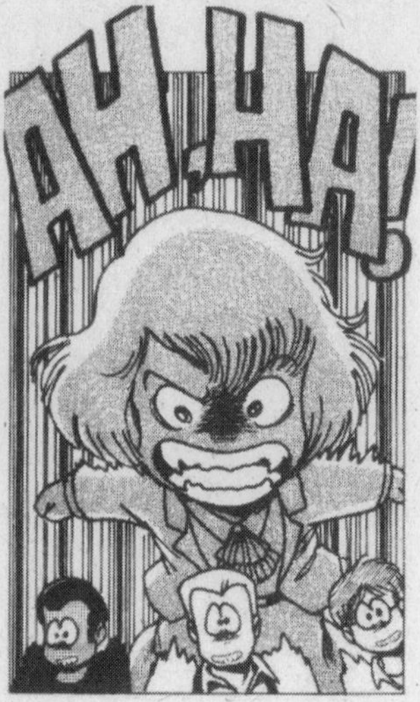
AH HA!

"AN UNPLEASANT DISCOVERY"

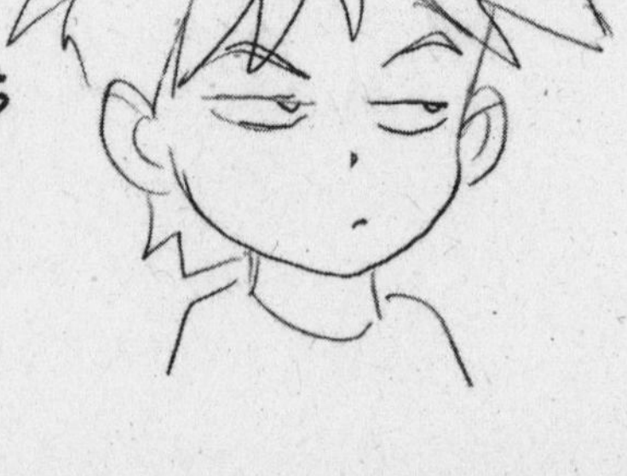

BOREDOM
MAKING SNIDE REMARKS
OR
INSINUATING

HOW TO DRAW MANGA

SMALL-BODIED TYPES
EXPRESSIONS

SCHEMING
AND
PLOTTING

HOPPING MAD
YELLING OUT LOUD

HOW TO DRAW MANGA

SMALL-BODIED TYPES
EXPRESSIONS

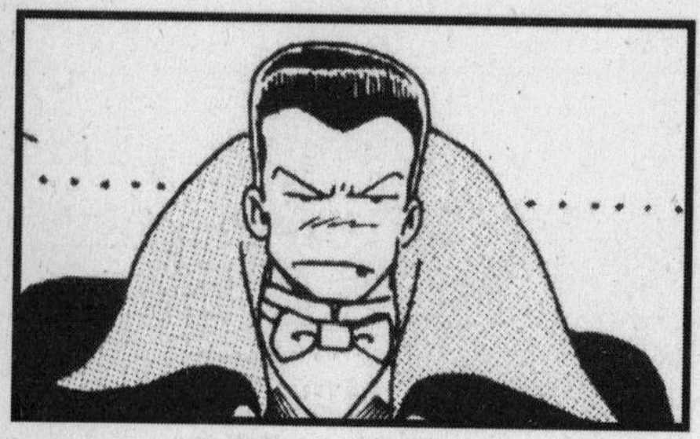

CONSTERNATION

VOWING
VENGEANCE!

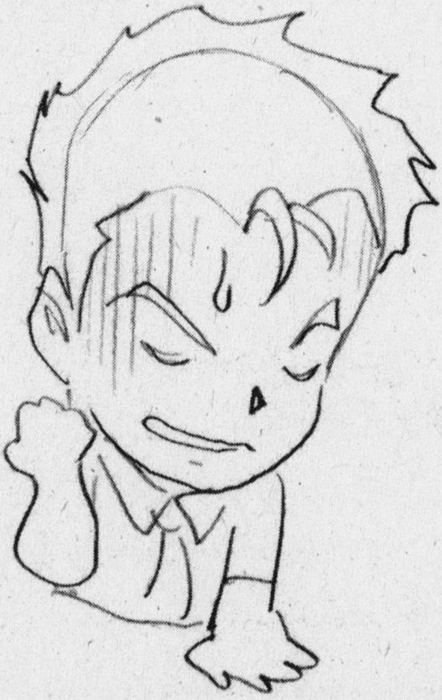

SMALL-BODIED TYPES
EXPRESSIONS

DRUNK WITH
POWER
OR...
HAVING
DELUSIONS
OF GRANDEUR!

BLATANT
REFUSAL

OR

DENIAL

SMALL-BODIED TYPES

EXPRESSIONS

POPPING EYES!

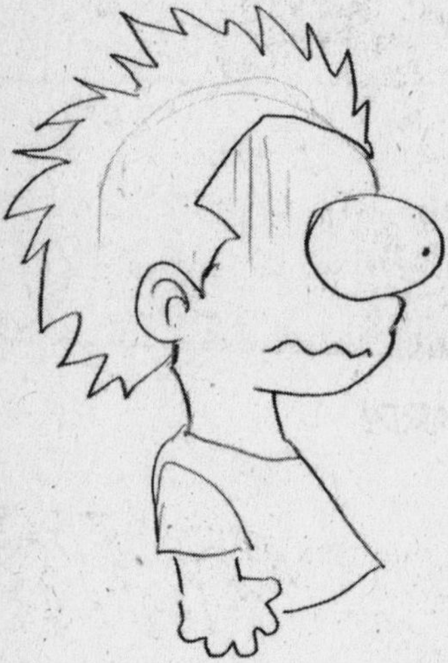

BUG
EYED
SURPRISE!

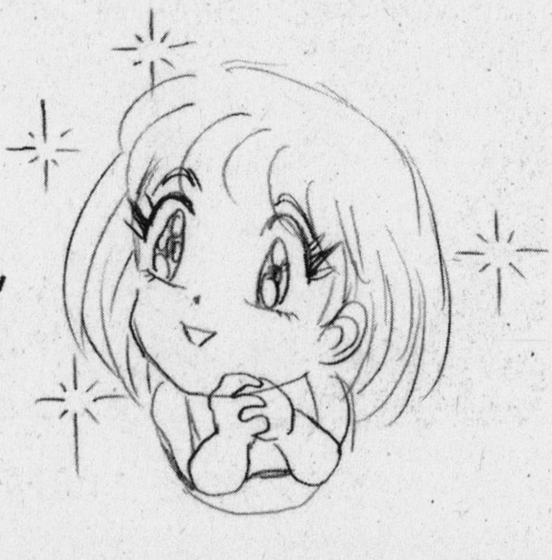

IN LOVE,
"BEING SWEET"
OR ENAMORED

HOW TO DRAW MANGA

SMALL-BODIED TYPES
EXPRESSIONS

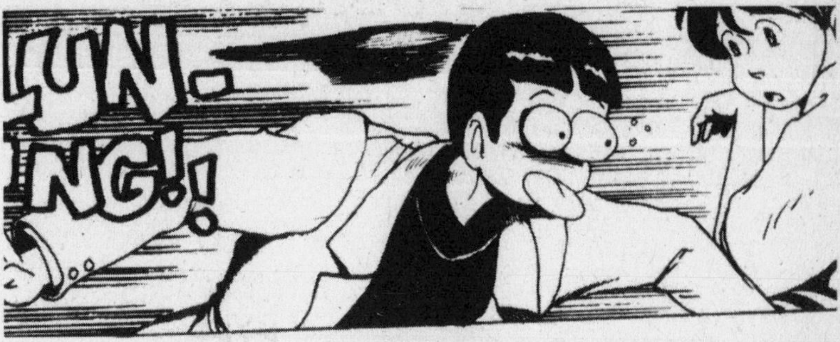

UN.
NG!!

CAUGHT OFF GUARD!

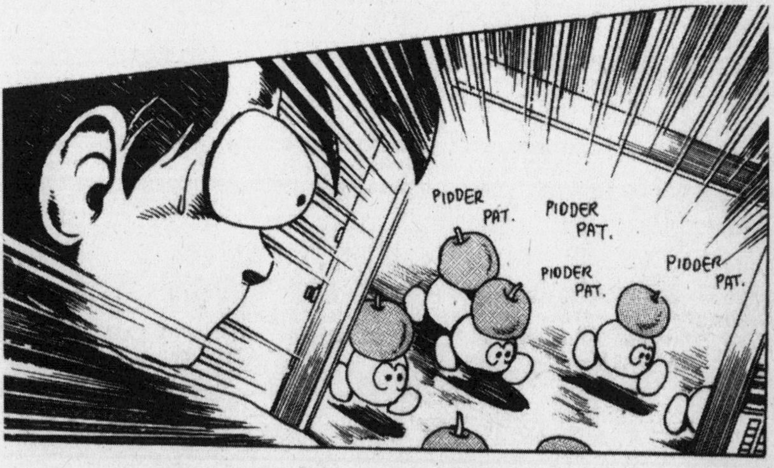

PIDDER PAT.
PIDDER PAT.
PIDDER PAT.
PIDDER PAT.

SHOCKING SURPRISE!

HOW TO DRAW MANGA

SMALL-BODIED TYPES
EXPRESSIONS

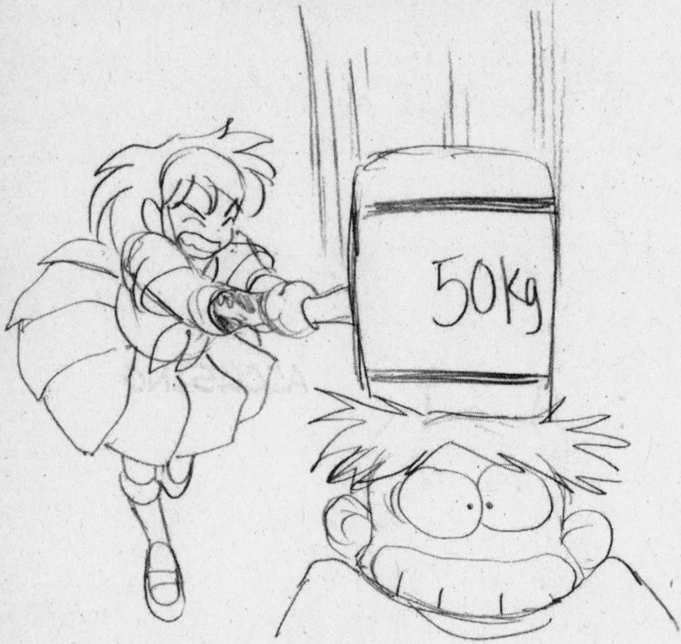

50Kg

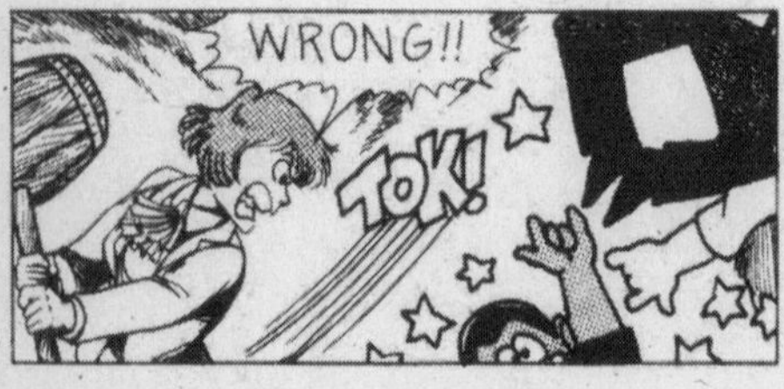

WRONG!!
TOK!

LARGE BUG EYED EXPRESSION COMBINED WITH THE LARGE TEETH IS A POPULAR EXPRESSION FOR PAIN IN MANGA.

HOW TO DRAW MANGA

SMALL-BODIED TYPES
EXPRESSIONS

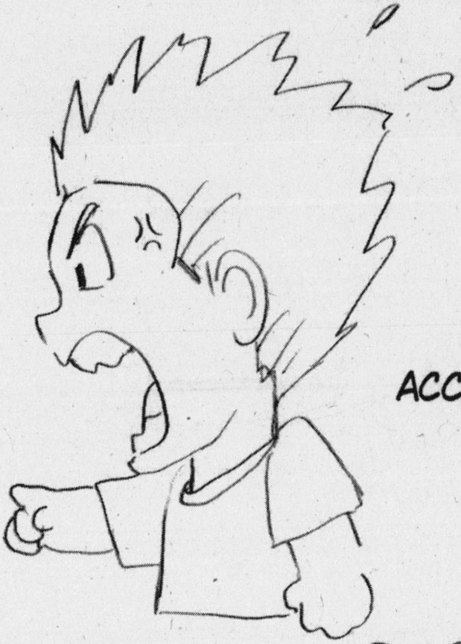
ACCUSING

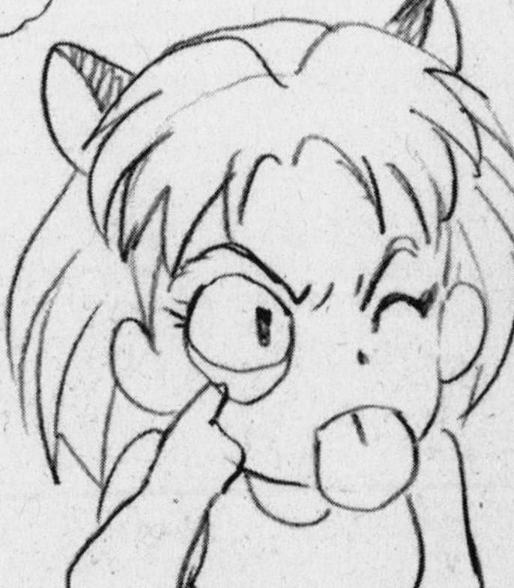
NYEEE!

PRACTICE PAGE

HOW TO DRAW MANGA

BASIC PERSPECTIVE

HORIZON LINE

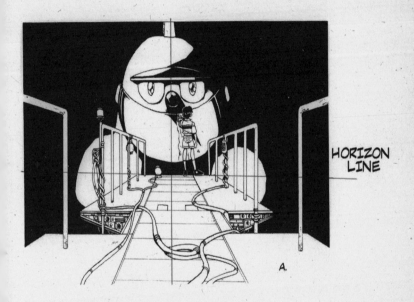

HORIZON LINE
A.

EXAMPLE A:
HERE I WANTED TO SHOW SCALE BETWEEN THE FOREGROUND OBJECT AND THE BACKGROUND OBJECT.

IMPORTANT NOTE TO REMEMBER: THE HORIZON LINE IS THE VERY FOUNDATION OF PERSPECTIVE. IT CAN BE A VERY POWERFUL TOOL IN DRAWING AND IS THE BASIS FOR ALL REALISTICALLY RENDERED DRAWING. IT WORKS IN FINE ART AS WELL AS IN MANGA, SO IT IS IMPORTANT TO MAKE NOTE OF IT!

HOW TO DRAW MANGA

BASIC PERSPECTIVE

HORIZON LINE

IN EXAMPLE B, DISTANCE IS WHAT I WAS AIMING FOR.

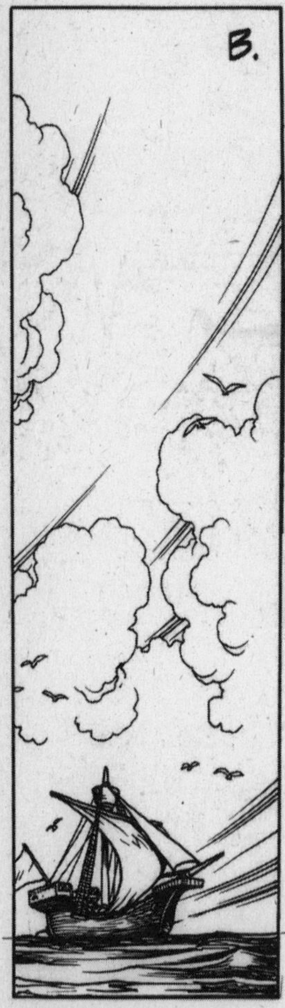
B.

EXAMPLE C SHOWS A CORRELATION BETWEEN OBJECTS IN THE FOREGROUND, THE MIDDLE GROUND AND THE BACKGROUND.

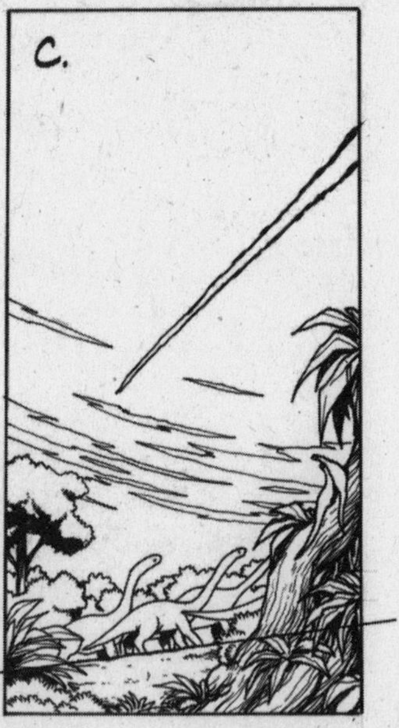
C.

HORIZON LINE

HOW TO DRAW MANGA

BASIC PERSPECTIVE

HORIZON LINE

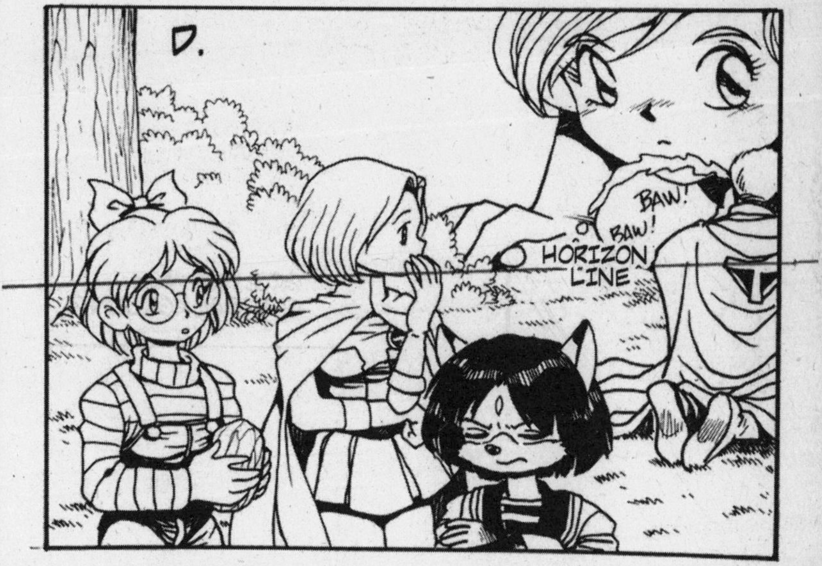
D.
BAW!
BAW!
HORIZON LINE

BY USING THE HORIZON LINE IN EXAMPLE D, YOU CAN ALSO USE A FORCED PERSPECTIVE.

BASIC PERSPECTIVE
HORIZON LINE

IN DRAWING, PERSPECTIVE IS IMPORTANT IN
REALISTIC ART OR DRAMATIC STORYTELLING.

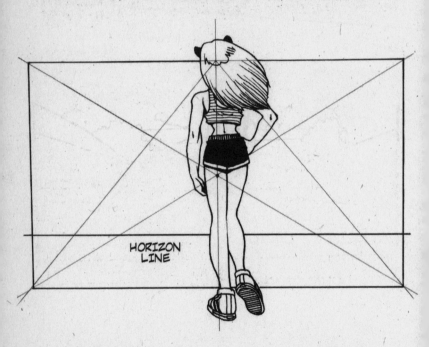

HORIZON
LINE

THE HORIZON LINE: THIS IS THE LINE THAT
APPEARS AS YOU LOOK OUT INTO THE DISTANT
HORIZON. IT SEPERATES LAND FROM SKY.

HOW TO DRAW MANGA

BASIC PERSPECTIVE
HORIZON LINE

NORMAL EYE VIEW

THIS HORIZON LINE IS ALWAYS THERE WHEN YOU STAND ON A LEVEL FIELD.
THIS LINE CAN BE BLOCKED BY OBJECTS OR DISTORTED BY LIGHT OR HEAT.

HORIZON
LINE

AT TIMES THE HORIZON WILL BE ONLY PARTLY VISABLE
AS IN THE ILLUSTRATION. IMAGINE THE HORIZON
LINE STRETCHING BEYOND THE OBSTRUCTIONS.

HOW TO DRAW MANGA

BASIC PERSPECTIVE
HORIZON LINE

IN PERSPECTIVE, IT IS IMPORTANT TO ESTABLISH THE VIEWER IN RELATION TO THE HORIZON LINE, AND IT SHOWS THE EYE LEVEL TO THE CHARACTER IN RELATION TO THE DRAWING.

Ⓐ

THE BIRD'S-EYE VIEW

THIS VIEW TAKES THE SUBJECT HIGH ABOVE THE GROUND. PLACING THE HORIZON HIGH ENABLES ONE TO SEE MORE OF THE GROUP. THE HIGHER THE HORIZON LINE, THE HIGHER THE VIEWPOINT. IT GIVES OBJECTS IN THE DISTANCE A SMALLER FEEL.

Ⓐ

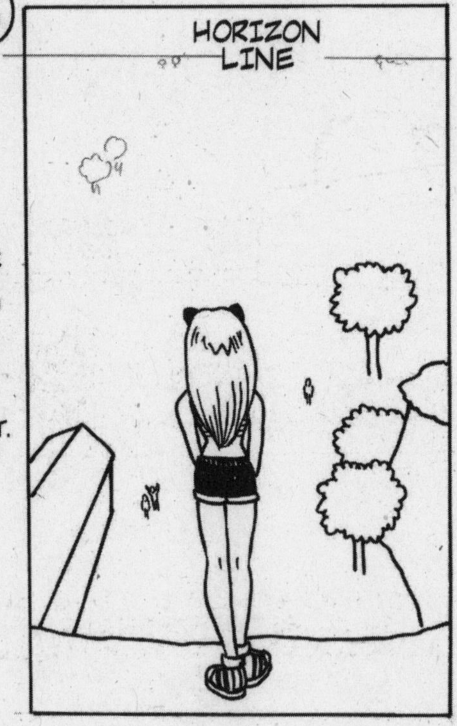
HORIZON LINE

BASIC PERSPECTIVE
POINT OF VIEW

(B) THE WORM'S-EYE VIEW

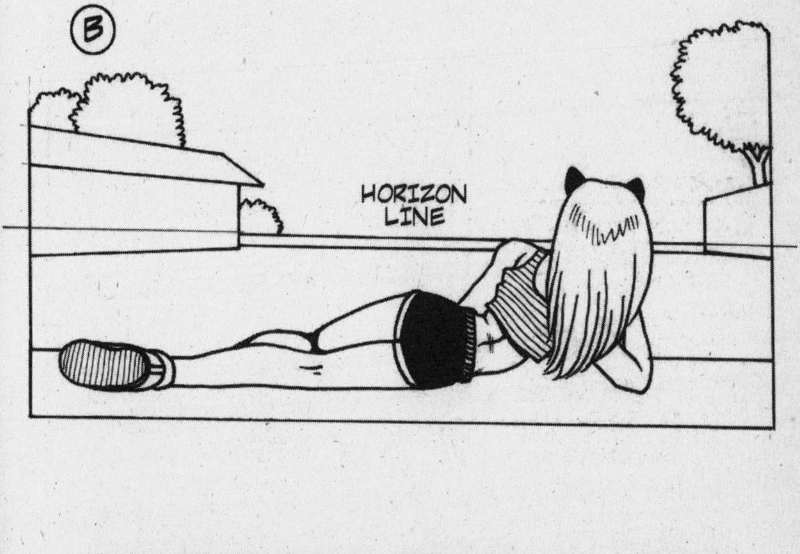
B
HORIZON LINE

THIS PERSPECTIVE IS USED WHEN THE SUBJECT IS CLOSE TO THE GROUND OR WAY BELOW THE HORIZON LINE. IT GIVES OBJECTS A LARGER FEEL.

HOW TO DRAW MANGA

BASIC PERSPECTIVE
POINT OF VIEW

EXAMPLES OF
BIRD'S-EYE VIEW
PERSPECTIVE...

USING THE BIRD'S-EYE
VIEW PERSPECTIVE GIVES
THE SPECTATOR A VISTA
OVER ALL THAT IS IN VIEW.
OFTEN IT IS USED TO
CONVEY VASTNESS,
SCALE AND TERRITORY.

HOW TO DRAW MANGA

BASIC PERSPECTIVE
POINT OF VIEW

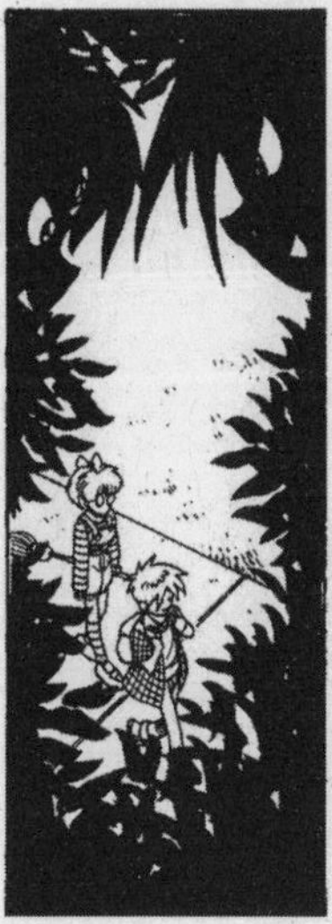

IT HELPS PLACE THE VIEWER IN AN AREA THAT HE CAN BECOME FAMILIAR WITH. IT ALSO GIVES CHARACTERS A SENSE OF PLACE.

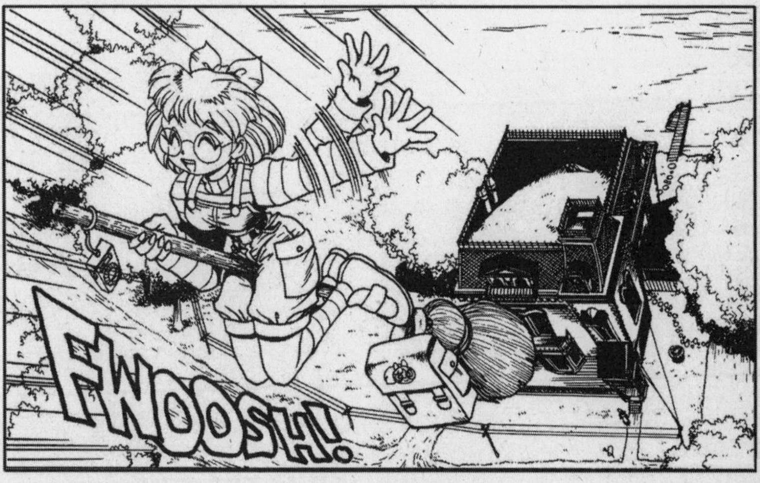
FWOOSH!

HOW TO DRAW MANGA

BASIC PERSPECTIVE
POINT OF VIEW

SIMPLE USE OF PERSPECTIVE
CAN HELP ESTABLISH TIME
AND PLACE. IT CAN GREATLY
INCREASE THE DRAMA OF ANY
GIVEN STORY.

HOW TO DRAW MANGA

BASIC PERSPECTIVE

PICTURE WINDOW

BEFORE MAKING A PERSPECTIVE DRAWING, YOU MUST IMAGINE WHAT IS CALLED A "PICTURE WINDOW." THIS IS THE IMAGINARY WINDOW BETWEEN THE SPECTATOR AND THE RENDERING.

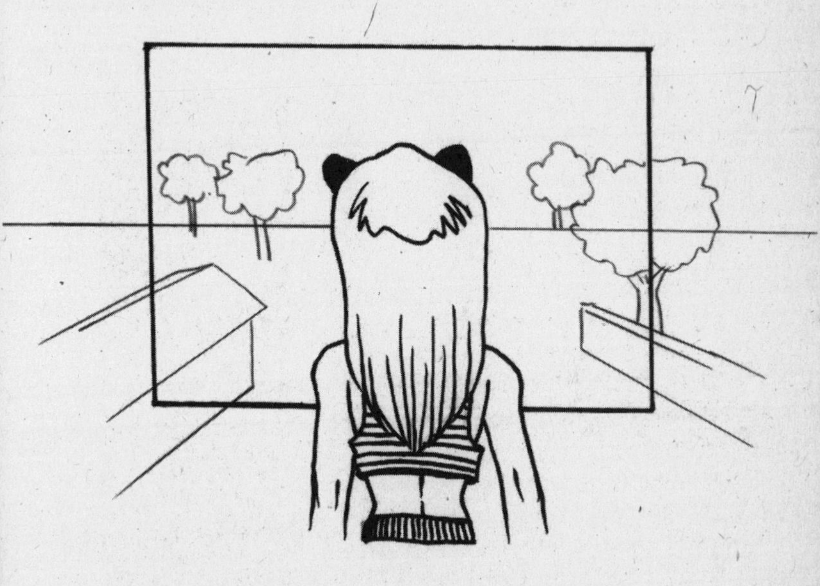

THIS ASPECT IS FUNDAMENTAL TO ALL OTHER ASPECTS OF PERSPECTIVE DRAWING.

BASIC PERSPECTIVE
LINE OF SIGHT

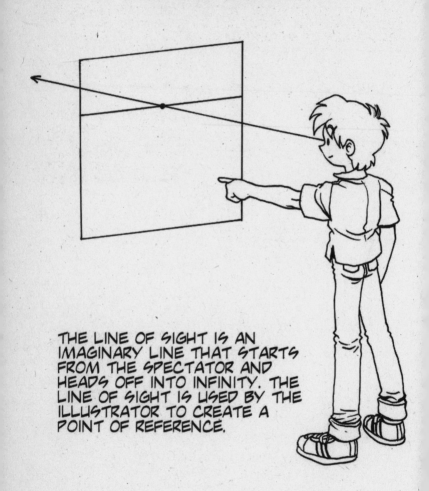

THE LINE OF SIGHT IS AN
IMAGINARY LINE THAT STARTS
FROM THE SPECTATOR AND
HEADS OFF INTO INFINITY. THE
LINE OF SIGHT IS USED BY THE
ILLUSTRATOR TO CREATE A
POINT OF REFERENCE.

BASIC PERSPECTIVE

IN ORDER TO MASTER PERSPECTIVE, IT IS IMPORTANT
TO KNOW WHAT IS BEING TALKED ABOUT. BELOW IS A
GLOSSARY OF STANDARD PERSPECTIVE TERMS.

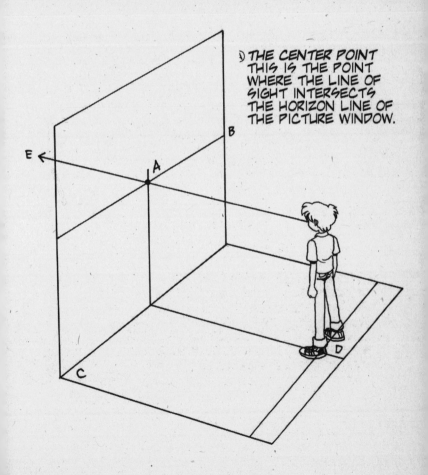

1) THE CENTER POINT
THIS IS THE POINT
WHERE THE LINE OF
SIGHT INTERSECTS
THE HORIZON LINE OF
THE PICTURE WINDOW.

BASIC PERSPECTIVE

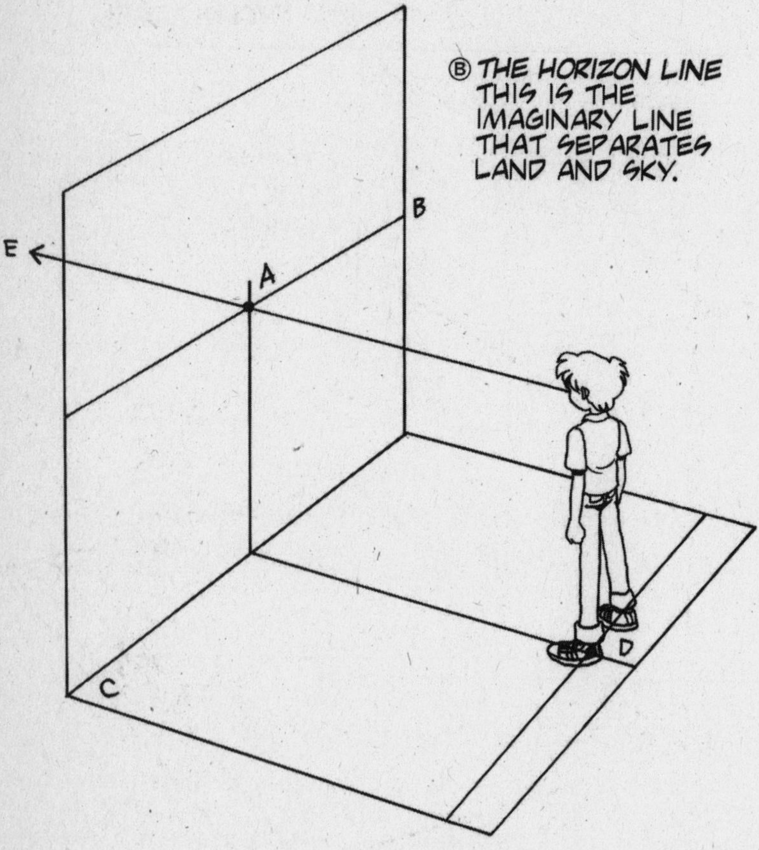
Ⓑ THE HORIZON LINE
THIS IS THE
IMAGINARY LINE
THAT SEPARATES
LAND AND SKY.
B
E
A
C
D

HOW TO DRAW MANGA

BASIC PERSPECTIVE

Ⓒ LAND LEVEL
THIS IS THE HORIZONTAL
LINE THAT SEPARATES
THE PICTURE WINDOW
AND GROUND LEVEL.

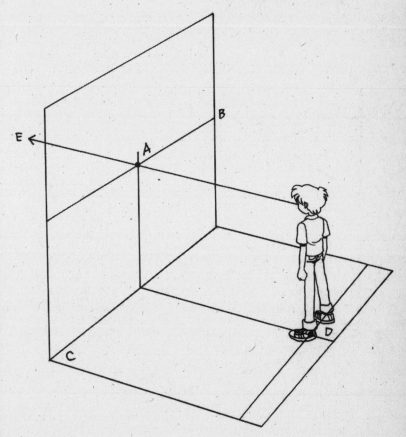

BASIC PERSPECTIVE

Ⓓ SPECTATOR POINT
    THIS IS THE POINT ON THE GROUND LEVEL
    WHERE THE SPECTATOR STANDS AND FROM
    WHICH THE LINE OF SIGHT STARTS.

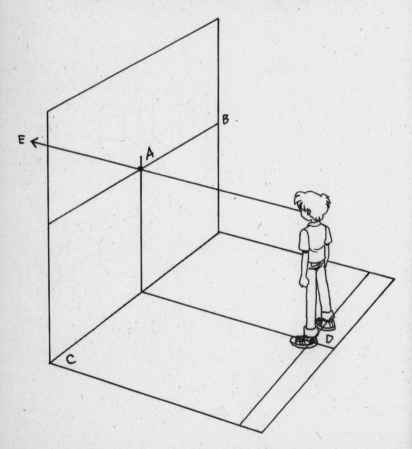

BASIC PERSPECTIVE
POINT OF VIEW

BY SWITCHING THE VIEWPOINT OF THE SPECTATOR,
AN OBJECT IN VIEW CAN BE CHANGED. THE CLOSER THE
VIEWER GETS TO AN OBJECT, THE MORE FORESHORTENING
(SEE SIDE BOX) APPEARS WITHOUT BASICALLY
ALTERING THE SIZE.

SPECTATOR VIEW   SPECTATOR DISTANCE

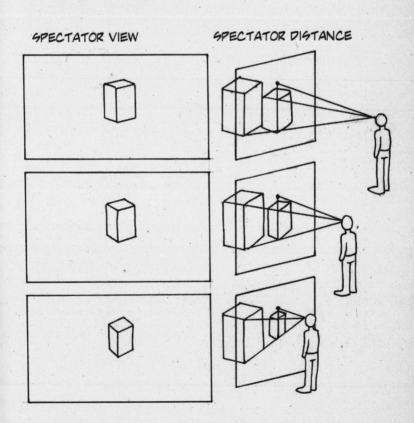

HOW TO DRAW MANGA

BASIC PERSPECTIVE
THE VANISHING POINT

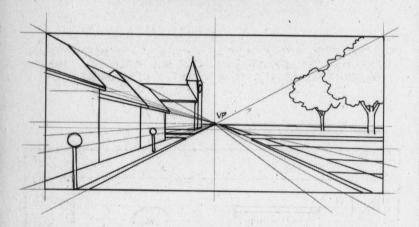

THE POINT ON THE LINE OF SIGHT WHERE ALL PARALLEL
LINES RECEDING FROM THE SPECTATOR CONVERGE IS
CALLED "THE VANISHING POINT." THIS IS THE POINT FROM
WHICH ALL LINES OF PERSPECTIVE START.

HOW TO DRAW MANGA

BASIC PERSPECTIVE
ONE POINT PERSPECTIVE

THE ONE POINT PERSPECTIVE IS THE MOST BASIC FORM OF DRAWN PERSPECTIVE IN THAT ALL PARALLEL LINES RETREATING FROM THE SPECTATOR CONVERGE AT A POINT KNOWN AS THE VANISHING POINT (VP).

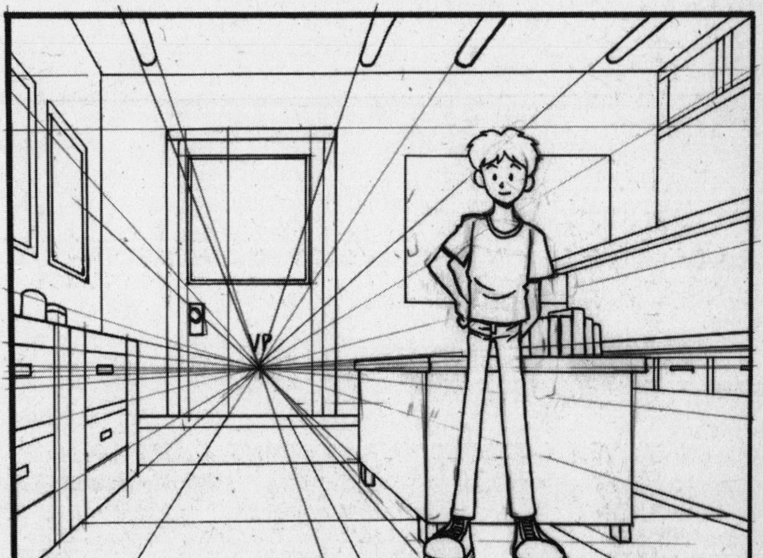
VP

HOW TO DRAW MANGA

BASIC PERSPECTIVE
ONE POINT PERSPECTIVE

ALL LINES AND PLANES THAT
ARE SQUARE ON, PARALLEL TO,
ON THE PICTURE PLANE (AND THE
OBSERVER) REMAIN PARALLEL AND TO THEIR
TRUE SHAPE WITHOUT DISTORTION OR FORESHORTENING.

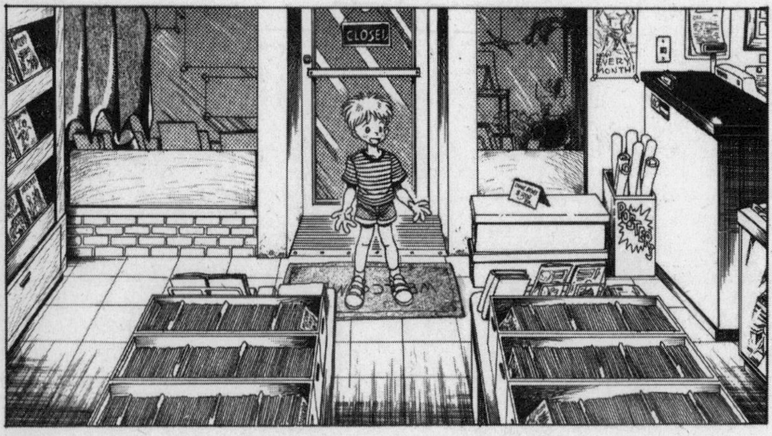
CLOSED
EVERY MONTH!

BASIC PERSPECTIVE
ABOVE AND BELOW

Ⓐ ABOVE THE HORIZONAL
LINE: FOR THOSE
OBJECTS THAT ARE
ABOVE THE OBSERVER'S
EYE LEVEL-- I.E.,
THE HORIZONTAL LINE.
THE VANISHING LINES
TRAVEL DOWNWARDS
TO THE CENTER OF
THE VANISHING POINT.

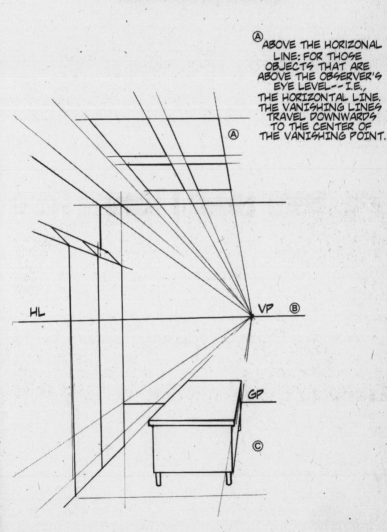

BASIC PERSPECTIVE
ABOVE AND BELOW

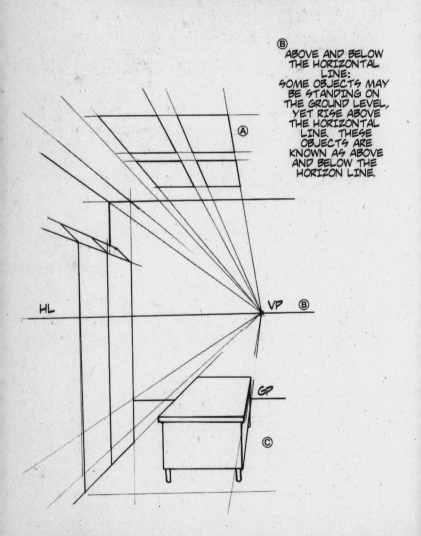

Ⓑ ABOVE AND BELOW
THE HORIZONTAL
LINE:
SOME OBJECTS MAY
BE STANDING ON
THE GROUND LEVEL,
YET RISE ABOVE
THE HORIZONTAL
LINE. THESE
OBJECTS ARE
KNOWN AS ABOVE
AND BELOW THE
HORIZON LINE.

Ⓐ

VP Ⓑ

HL

GP

Ⓒ